FREEDOM AND PROVIDENCE

IS VOLUME

22

OF THE

Twentieth Century Encyclopedia of Catholicism

UNDER SECTION

II

*THE BASIC TRUTHS*

IT IS ALSO THE

49TH

VOLUME IN ORDER OF PUBLICATION

*Edited by HENRI DANIEL-ROPS of the Académie Française*

# FREEDOM
# AND PROVIDENCE

*By MARK PONTIFEX, O.S.B.*

**HAWTHORN BOOKS · PUBLISHERS ·** *New York*

*First Edition,* September, 1960

NIHIL OBSTAT

Johannes M. T. Barton, S.T.D., L.S.S.

*Censor Deputatus*

IMPRIMATUR

E. Morrogh Bernard

*Vicarius Generalis*

Westmonasterii, die XIII APRILIS MCMLX

# CONTENTS

INTRODUCTION     7

I. MAN'S POWER OF FREE CHOICE     9
Meaning of Man's Freedom     9
The Meaning of Free Choice     12
    Arguments against Free Choice     12
    Arguments for Free Choice     14
Christians Committed to Free Choice     15

II. OUR KNOWLEDGE OF GOD     18
Existence of the Absolutely Perfect     18
The Absolutely Perfect and the First Cause     20
Implications     24

III. GOD'S LOVE AND PROVIDENCE     30
Meaning of God's Knowledge     30
Meaning of God's Will     32
God's Freedom and Necessity     35
God's Love for Creatures     39
Creatures' Love for God     42

IV. EVIL     48
How Can Evil Be Compatible with God's
    Providence?     48
The Meaning of Evil     50
The Meaning of God's Omnipotence     52
The Meaning of God's Goodness     54
Limits to the Perfection Which God Can Give
    to Creatures     56
The Possibility of Evil Inherent in Creation     59
Animal Pain     61

V. SIN      64
     The Molinist Solution      65
     The Thomist Solution      66
     A Proposal      68

VI. THE PROPOSED SOLUTION      70
     Choice Lies between a Greater and a Lesser
       Good      70
     Choice between Good and Evil      73
     Answers to Certain Objections      77
     Why Does God Give the Creature the Power
       of Free Choice      80

VII. SOME FURTHER QUESTIONS      83

VIII. PUNISHMENT      93
     Pain, Purposeless in Itself, May Indirectly
       Serve a Good Purpose      93
     St. Thomas' Theory of Punishment      95
     Punishment and Mercy      99
     Conclusions about Punishment      102
     Applications of These Conclusions      103

CONCLUSIONS      110
     Summary of the Argument      110
     Predestination      111
     The Question of Miracles      113
     The Right Attitude to God's Providence      114
     Prayer and Providence      118
     Freedom      118

EPILOGUE      122

SELECT BIBLIOGRAPHY      137

# INTRODUCTION

I should like to warn the reader at once that he cannot expect a book on God's providence to be very easy to read. Of its very nature the subject is one in which the imagination has little scope; it is almost wholly a matter of argument. To try to popularize the subject, in the sense of trying to make it easy reading, would be inevitably to leave the real subject aside and to talk of something else. For an explanation of God's providence in connection with human freedom means principally a discussion of the problem of their reconciliation, and this is necessarily a somewhat intricate and abstract process, though of course immensely important for Christian apologetics and of fascinating interest for its own sake. The only way in which the subject can be made at all easy is by making the argument clear. This I have done my best to keep in mind, and have tried to make all the terms used comprehensible to any reader without special training.

The plan of the book follows, I think, naturally from the subject. The Vatican Council declares: "God upholds and governs by his providence everything that he has made, reaching from end to end mightily and ordering all things sweetly (cf. Wisdom 8. 1). For 'all things are naked and open to his eyes' (Hebrew 4. 13), those things, too, which are to come about through the free action of creatures" (Denzinger, *Enchiridion Symbolorum*, 1784). So the first thing is to discuss what is meant by freedom and free choice. Then we must examine our knowledge of God. We find that God is the infinitely perfect first cause, living in the eternal present. We find, too, that he knows and loves his creatures, and desires their final happiness. Where, then, is the problem? Is not God's loving providence and predestination of his creatures easy to explain? In fact, however, the world is not as we should expect, for on every side there is evil. Moreover, how can the creature choose freely, if God is the supreme Lord? Therefore a theory must be suggested to meet these problems, first, with regard to evil in general, and, then, with regard to evil caused by the creature's free choice. A special problem is raised by the pain of punishment, and so next I turn to that. The final chapter sums up the argument, and tries to show that human personality can be free in the most important sense, and also entirely dependent on God.

I should mention in conclusion that a number of passages in the book are taken from articles I have written at different times for *The Downside Review*.

# CHAPTER I

# MAN'S POWER OF FREE CHOICE

Even the largest book would be far too small for a full discussion of God's providence over his creatures, and here only a mere outline can be attempted. Very many objections have been raised against the teaching of the Church, and they have been answered in very many different ways. In the space available here I think my best plan is, for the most part, simply to use the line of argument which seems to me personally the best for meeting the difficulties. I shall mention shortly other theories which have been put forward to defend the Christian view, but shall not be able to deal with them at length.

## *MEANING OF MAN'S FREEDOM*

Let us begin, then, by asking what is meant when we speak of a man's being free. Freedom means the absence of constraint or hindrance; it implies that some force or tendency is seeking to exert itself, and that nothing is preventing it from doing so. Now what are the powers which a man has, and which may or may not exert themselves without hindrance? The special characteristic of man, as opposed to other things in the world around us, is that he is aware of himself and of his environment far more fully than is anything else. As a result of this awareness he is conscious of his needs and tendencies on many levels, and so, instead of being mere blind forces, they become for him conscious desires. Hence, man has feelings and emotions of many kinds. How far do man's desires extend? As we all know, some people think that man is only aware of physical things, that is, of things in time and space. Others think, as do Christians, that in and through physical things he is also aware of things that are not subject to the limitations of time and space. They think, for example, that he is aware of himself and of other men as being in some measure free from these limitations, and that he is also aware of God, the ultimate source of all things. In any case this can be said: man has the power, not only to be aware of himself as affected by external objects, and of external objects as affecting himself, but also to analyse, clarify, and classify the objects which he knows. By these means he can develop his knowledge of other things and of himself. Man, then, is a being with bodily powers by which he can seek to maintain his body and enjoy its use and to help others to do the same, and with powers of the mind by which he can seek to understand his environment and enjoy it, to get rid of obstacles and develop his powers, and also to help others to do the same. In order to achieve this he can train himself in habits which will enable him to use his powers more easily and effectively. Virtues are habits which tend towards man's perfection, while vices are habits which tend against his perfection.

Man is not merely an isolated individual, but is a member of human society. On the one hand he should develop his individual personality, and on the other hand he should do this for the good of other men, if he is to develop his own powers fully. First, as to his individual personality. To appreciate what this implies we have only to think of the way in which a child should not be educated. If it were possible to put a child to sleep and repeat facts to it, so that it would acquire a great deal of information without any trouble and with great accuracy, this might perhaps have some useful purpose but it would not be education. A human being should be the true agent of his acts, and should make his knowledge his own. He should, of course, be passive so far as to have material on which to act, but he should himself act upon this material, put its elements into relation with one another, and see for himself what is implied. There would be no progress in perfection unless men were active centres of thought, and unless this led to external good conduct. The ultimate reason why this is true is, to the Christian, that each creature is intended to reflect and reveal God's perfection in a way which is, to some extent, unique, and that this can only be achieved if each creature is, under God, a primary source of activity. The individual must not, therefore, be merely passive to outside influences, a mere instrument in their hands, but must develop his own personality and initiate activity himself.

Secondly, there is the social aspect to consider. While man must develop his individual personality, if he is to perfect his powers, he can never do this in isolation. He depends on his fellow men for his own perfection, just as they depend on him. He must be a source of activity, but this activity must aim at the good of all mankind. Unless he works for this end, and is able himself to enjoy the good of all, man has not reached the full enjoyment of his individual powers.

With these remarks in mind we can now go on to fill in the picture of man's freedom. Man can be called free in all the different ways in which his powers seek to exert themselves. He is free in one sense if his bodily powers are able to act unhindered, and this again may happen in many different ways. He is free in another sense if his intellectual powers are able to act unhindered. Lack of education and training is plainly a hindrance as well as lack of the information he needs. Again a man is free in another sense if he acts in obedience to reason rather than passion, for then he acts in such a way as to reach a more important end. It is not difficult to think of many other ways in which a man may be called free, on the ground that his powers, in one combination or another, or in one aspect or another, act unhindered. It follows that he is only free in the fullest sense if all his powers have reached their fullest development, and are able to act in their highest intensity. Plainly this can never happen in the present life, but only in the next life through enjoyment of the beatific vision.

## THE MEANING OF FREE CHOICE

Finally, we come to the question of free choice. Man is often called free in the sense that he is said to be able to choose between two or more courses of action without being forced to choose one or other by anything except his own will. If this is so, he is free because his power of action is not determined by objects outside himself; his power to act in one way or another is under his own control and, therefore, free.

This brings us to the familiar controversy as to whether man really has this power of choice, or whether it is an illusion, his actions being determined really by causes outside his personal will. I shall summarize the main arguments on each side.

### Arguments against free choice

The determinist relies chiefly on showing that man's actions can be explained by causes which seem quite adequate, without bringing in free choice. There can be no doubt that on the surface the determinist has a strong case. If we are asked why a man acted in a particular way we tend at once to assume that he did so because he had a certain type of character. But there can be no doubt that character, at least to a large extent, is inherited and depends on physical causes. Moreover, different nations have types of character peculiar to themselves, and many actions are traceable to this cause. The line of argument is specially emphasized by statistics. These show that a great many actions occur with a regularity which suggests that causes other than free choice have produced them. When statistics show, for example, a steady increase in crimes of violence we look at once to social changes as an explanation rather than to free choice. And, if it is due to free choice, why do the number of crimes follow a fairly steady curve? Hastings Rashdall in *The Theory of Good and Evil* (vol. 2, p. 317) says: "Indeterminism . . would never even occur to a scientifically trained mind acquainted with such facts as I have mentioned and accustomed to deal with social and psychological phenomena, unless it were in the first instance suggested by ethical or religious considerations." Rashdall goes on to point out further objections to indeterminism. He says that, if we take indeterminism in its extreme form, we shall have to abstract all that a man owes to inherited character or to the influence of others, before we can call him good or bad.

> The only really logical form of such extreme Indeterminism would carry with it (as it did avowedly for Kant) the startling consequence that no man can really be made better by the influence of another. A mode of thinking which compels us to deny the sanctity of St Paul because it might never have existed but for the influence of Christ, of St Augustine because it would not have existed but for St Ambrose . . . is more flatly opposed to the deepest moral convictions of mankind than the crudest and most mechanical theory of human conduct by which Determinism has ever been caricatured. (P. 322.)

Then Rashdall argues that, if we pursue this line of thought which an extreme form of indeterminism might be expected to follow, we shall have to treat as good all the people who might have been good under good influence, however bad in fact they are. What he means is that, if goodness depends entirely on a man's free choice and if this can be decisively affected by good influence, a man ought to be regarded as good if we think he would have become good had he been subjected to a sufficiently powerful good influence.

One point should be noticed here which Rashdall makes and which seems undeniable, namely, that a man may act from the highest motives and yet not be acting from free choice. His act may be fully determined by causes outside his own will, and yet his act may be a fully personal act, and a good act. For he may have no desire but to do the right thing, and may act on the motive of this desire with full deliberation and awareness of the purpose in view. To be free from all desire for wrong is surely a perfection, and therefore to wish only to do right can imply no lack of goodness. But there can be no possibility of choice if there is no conflict of desire, and hence an act done without any choice may be done solely from the highest motive, the desire for good, and it may fully express the individual personality. After all this must happen when a creature enjoys the beatific vision, for then the creature is faced with an object clearly able to satisfy every possible desire, and a contrary desire would be inconceivable.

## Arguments for free choice

These, then, are some of the arguments which can be brought against the belief that man has the power to choose freely. Now let us glance at the arguments on the other side. Perhaps the chief of these is simply the claim which many men, probably most men, would make that at times they are directly and clearly aware of their power to choose. For example, they would feel sure that on certain occasions they have the power either to make a little more effort to carry out some purpose, or not to make it. Whatever difficulties may follow from this conviction, it seems to them so clear that it must be treated as a starting point for discussion. To deny this seems to them to involve greater difficulties than are involved in asserting it.

Again, this view appears to be supported by the instinctive way in which mankind acts, in spite of the well-known arguments against free choice. Men have always been accustomed to regard some good acts and some bad acts as done from free choice. A court of law carries out its work in quite a different spirit from a group of doctors. At least, in common opinion punishment is not the same as the healing of disease.

Again, a sense of responsibility is usually regarded as an important virtue, and it is very hard to see what can be meant by the realization of responsibility, if all our acts are wholly determined by causes outside ourselves. Of course, it may be argued that all it means is that we ought to have the right desires and intentions, but, if it only means this and nothing more, if it does not mean that we ourselves can in some degree determine our desires, then responsibility has not been explained but explained away. Yet the fact remains that most people would suppose it had a real meaning of its own. So, too, remorse is a feeling which most men have, yet, unless there is free choice, it must be baseless.

Finally, there is this point: how do we come to discuss whether we really have free choice, if there is no such thing? How did the idea, or the mistaken notion that there was such an idea, ever arise, if there was nothing whatever in reality to justify it?

From the point of view of natural reason alone there are, then, undoubtedly strong arguments on both sides, and, leaving out the authority of the Church, all that could be said is that everyone must make up his mind for himself. But there can be no question about the judgement of the Church. The fact of sin, that is to say, of wrong done by free choice, lies at the root of Christianity. Original sin would have no meaning in Christian doctrine, if it had been brought about by irresistible causes. The whole doctrine and practice of forgiveness of sins presupposes that they have been committed by free choice. For the Christian, or in any case for the Catholic, the matter is undoubtedly settled.

## CHRISTIANS COMMITTED TO FREE CHOICE

So the doctrine of the Church commits us to belief in free choice, in indeterminism of some kind, and we see that there are good reasons, apart from Christian faith, which support this belief. But can we meet the objections against it? I think to a large extent we can. We must remember that, though we are committed to accepting the fact of free choice, there is wide scope for discussion about how and when it takes place. Manifestly, in view of statistics and of the physical causes which determine conduct, we must narrow the field of free choice, and not apply it to every human action in its entirety. Very many kinds of human action are clearly produced by causes other than free choice, and the problem is to see how we can plausibly find space for it. Perhaps the best suggestion is to argue that we are very frequently capable of making by our free choice some effort, however slight, in a certain direction, that is to say, of focusing our attention on a given end and acting accordingly in some degree, or of not doing so. A particular man at a particular time may not be capable of fully determining for himself the external act in question, but he may be capable of some degree of effort towards determining it. For example, a criminal may have inherited a character of low intelligence and strong tendencies to evil, and all this may have been made worse by his environment. When a temptation to crime comes it may not be in his power to make such a strong effort that he will refrain from it, but it may be in his power to make some effort. If this is so, all that the statistics show is that certain causes, arising from circumstances and physical facts, occur regularly; this will be no more remarkable than the regularity of any other physical facts. They do not show how often some freely chosen effort is made or omitted, or its degree of intensity. There may have been no possibility that this would show itself in outward act, and so statistics omit it altogether. Of course such a theory would not imply that free choice never causes outward acts, but only that this does not occur so often as might be expected. Moreover, we may suppose that some people can exercise free choice far more easily than others. After all it is commonly agreed that training and education have as part of their purpose to develop self-control, that is to say, the power of the individual person to exercise free choice in the right direction.

Some such theory as this seems to help us to meet the objections which are drawn from the undoubted physical causes which often determine conduct, and to leave room for free choice. Rashdall admits that his arguments do not disprove free choice, though he says, "Granted that an inmost kernel of undetermined action exists, it is something which is wholly inaccessible to human observation" (p. 323). This seems far too sweeping. I should agree that free choice is not nearly so visible in external conduct as might at first sight be expected, but I should hold that it is visible fairly frequently in some men at certain times, and that even the unsuccessful effort made to resist an overwhelming physical tendency may show in outward signs.

There are also the other objections to indeterminism which arise from the apparent absurdities to which it may seem to lead: that a man's real virtue or vice lies in that element alone which his free choice contributes to his conduct, and that, therefore, all that is due to the influence of others must be omitted if we are to estimate his conduct truly. I think an answer can be made to this, but it will be better to leave it until later on, when we consider the problems connected with God's providence and free choice.

In this chapter, then, we have seen what is meant by freedom as it applies to man. Some of the chief arguments for and against free choice have been considered, and we have seen that the Church's teaching involves acceptance of it as a real fact, even though it may not show itself in outward action so clearly as might be thought likely. We are faced with another set of problems when we reflect on the relationship between a creature who can choose freely and an almighty, all-good, God. To prepare the way for discussing these problems we must consider shortly the kind of knowledge we have of God, so as to get a right idea of the nature of the question.

# CHAPTER II

# OUR KNOWLEDGE OF GOD

Most people would agree that what man is aware of is himself as affected by external things and external things as affecting himself. The question is: what are these external things; how far does man's awareness stretch? Does it only go as far as the things perceived by the senses, or does it reach, in and through these sensible objects, that which is absolutely perfect, that than which nothing greater can be conceived? Manifestly, everyone is not clearly and explicitly aware of such an object, for many would strongly deny it. But the question is whether they are aware of it implicitly, that is to say, whether the confused datum of awareness which we have to work at by means of reflection and which we have to analyse and make explicit, contains the absolutely perfect or does not do so.

## THE EXISTENCE OF THE ABSOLUTELY PERFECT

Let us start from the fact that we can at least ask this question. But, if we can ask this question, does it not imply that the idea of the absolutely perfect has meaning for us? And, if this is so, how can we have obtained the idea except from that which is absolutely perfect? Does it not follow at once that the absolutely perfect, which we call God, exists, and that we have some knowledge of him? We cannot invent entirely new ideas; we can only rearrange material, which really exists and which we have known, into fresh patterns. Experience shows us this. But no rearrangement of imperfect, finite, material can make up the absolutely perfect, the infinite. May we not, therefore, argue that we have a true idea of the absolutely perfect, and hence that the absolutely perfect really exists? How else can we explain the undoubted fact that we can talk about it?

There are obvious objections to this argument, and they centre round the question: have we really an idea of the absolutely perfect? Does this really have any meaning for us? It may be said that, when we suppose ourselves to be thinking of absolute perfection, all we are doing is to think of a degree of perfection beyond any particular degree we may have experienced, but that this does not imply absolute perfection. Absolute perfection would not be a gradually advancing perfection, endlessly increasing in intensity, but a perfection which could not ever be reached by any advancing degree of perfection, however far it went, a perfection beyond any degree that we can ever directly conceive. The only possible reply to the objection consists in pointing to the objection itself. The objection says that we do not really have an idea of absolute perfection, because the idea of absolute perfection goes beyond anything we conceive of. But does not this imply that absolute perfection does have meaning for us? How else can the objection be explained? If we can ask whether we really attach meaning to absolute perfection, or indeed if we can deny that this is possible, it seems that we must attach meaning to it. Otherwise why should we wonder whether any limited degree, however great, is the most that we can conceive? Of course everyone would agree that we cannot conceive of absolute perfection fully and directly, that we can only do so indirectly, in and through and beyond any finite degree of perfection on which we can fix our minds, in the background of our field of consciousness.

To this, however, it will be answered that in any case absolute perfection is contradictory and, therefore, cannot have any meaning. When we call a thing perfect we mean that its powers or purposes are fully realized, that its appropriate activity is fully developed. A perfect flower would be a flower whose appropriate form of activity was fully realized, and in which there were no powers left undeveloped, possible to that kind of flower at that period of its growth. A picture or statue would be perfect so far as the materials out of which it was made had acquired a form capable of giving pleasure of the right kind to those who looked at it.

But, if this is so, is not absolute perfection contradictory? An absolutely perfect thing would be a thing whose own appropriate activity, whose own purpose and powers, were fully realized, and in whose own activity was included the activity of everything else. For, if it did not include all kinds of perfection, it would be to this extent limited and not absolutely perfect. But how is this conceivable? Are not many kinds of perfection incompatible with one another, and is not each thing necessarily limited to its own kind of perfection, so that the purpose and perfection of a flower necessarily excludes that of a stone? Is not, then, the idea of an absolutely perfect thing contradictory?

## THE ABSOLUTELY PERFECT AND THE FIRST CAUSE

Clearly it would be if the absolutely perfect thing were of the same order of being as imperfect things, and if perfect and imperfect could be directly compared. But, if the absolutely perfect thing is the first cause on which all imperfect things depend, then the conclusion does not follow. For, if there is a first cause, the very fact that all finite things depend upon it implies that in a true sense it includes in itself all finite perfections. Since the first cause is able to produce these perfections, it must in a true sense possess these as included in its own appropriate perfection. Moreover, it is no limitation to the first cause that it does not possess the perfections of its effects in the way in which the effects possess them, because what is wholly derived from the cause cannot add anything to the cause. In other words, finite things must be incomparable in any direct sense with the first cause, since there can be no common element to form a ground for comparison. Finite and infinite are in different orders of being, one entirely cause, the other entirely effect.

Thus I am arguing that an absolutely perfect thing would be such as to include all perfections, yet that this would not be contradictory, if the absolutely perfect thing were the first cause and the source of all perfections. Though finite perfections are often incompatible with one another, and one finite thing cannot possess the perfection of another, nevertheless, if there is a first cause, this must in a true, though different, sense possess them all since they are wholly derived from their source.

There seems no reason, then, to say that our idea of the absolutely perfect is meaningless because it involves contradiction. Provided that we regard the absolutely perfect as the source of all other perfections the objection can be met. The claim is that we can talk about the absolutely perfect cause of everything, and that this idea has meaning for us, and that we could not have such an idea unless we had derived it in some way from that which is absolutely perfect and really exists.

It may be interesting to add another argument, which tends to show that, if imperfect finite things exist then the perfect and infinite thing must exist as their cause. Thus it links the absolutely perfect with the first cause.

The argument is this. I experience something, in the relationship, for instance, between my fingers and my pen, which I call activity. Activity is not simply identical with any particular act because it is to be found in every act. Everything that is known or knowable is active, because it is only by acting upon me that I can know it. Activity or energy, which are the same as reality or being, are common, therefore, to everything, and there is nothing to which they do not apply. Inactivity is simply nothing.

Now this leads to a problem. If activity is common to everything it seems that it will be the supreme genus, but this is impossible. As we classify things under more general headings we focus our minds on a more and more indeterminate element which is held in common. We think of lions and tigers, and class them together as animals by focusing our minds on what is common to them both, but is indeterminate to either lions or tigers. If we carry on this process we might expect to come in the end to that which is common to absolutely everything, and is therefore completely indeterminate. In fact, however, the absolutely indeterminate would be meaningless because it would be mere passivity. What we do come to, and find common to everything, is activity or energy, the very opposite of passivity. Activity cannot, however, be the supreme genus because, being common to absolutely everything, there can be nothing other than it to differentiate it. Tiger is differentiated from lion by an element which we do not include in "animal". But activity is all-inclusive, since the completely inactive is non-existent, or meaningless.

What, then, are we to say? I suggest the following argument. I am aware of my fingers pressing against a pen, I find that, when I am aware of this, I am aware of something in the relationship of my fingers to the pen, which I call activity. It cannot be identical with any particular thing, because it is present in everything I experience, mental as well as physical. Then I reflect on what activity implies. I am confronted with a multitude of things, each of which is active in a different way, that is to say, in a restricted or limited way. I ask myself what I am aware of, when I am aware of these limited kinds of activity. How can activity be limited, when it is all-inclusive and inactivity is nothing? Activity cannot be the supreme genus, an absolutely universal class which includes everything.

A clue to the problem is given when we think of the meaning of activity. An agent acts on a patient, and a patient receives what an agent gives. A limited activity is a particular kind of activity, and this cannot be the same as pure activity, nor can it be a modification of pure activity, since pure activity cannot be modified, for it is active and not passive. But limited activity can be the effect of pure activity. It can be explained as activity received from pure activity, or (what comes to the same) as a possible kind of activity made actual. This explanation seems to satisfy the requirements and to make sense, and there does not seem any other which does so. Therefore I conclude that, when I am aware of the activity of the pen, I am not aware of this limited activity by itself alone, but am aware of it as derived from that which is pure activity. Hence I conclude that the first cause, which is pure activity, really exists.

It may help to explain what I mean if I put the argument in a slightly different form. The suggestion is that, whenever we are aware of a thing with limited activity, that is, with a particular kind of activity, we are in fact aware of a twofold object, of an effect and of a cause, of something which, by its very character as a particular or limited kind of activity, is passive to the action of that which is wholly active. Active, therefore, has a narrower and a wider meaning. Taken in its full scope it includes infinite activity, and hence, taken in its full scope activity cannot be limited. But although activity implies a double object, effect-implying-cause, and although we cannot think of effect and cause in complete isolation from one another, nevertheless we can focus our attention on each separately. When we focus our attention on the effect, on activity as received from the first cause, then we are aware of limited activity. When we focus our attention on the cause, then we are aware of pure, unlimited, activity. We use the word "activity" of both, but this does not mean that there is a common element, activity, which is modified in different ways in cause and effect. The cause is absolutely simple, and cannot be modified at all. The limited effect is unlike the cause except in so far as, being wholly derived from the cause, its perfection is contained in the cause. It is for this reason that we use the same word, activity, of both, but it is only used partly in the same sense and partly in a different sense.

Thus, when we classify things in more and more general

classes, instead of coming to an absolutely general class, which would be meaningless, we come to the single first cause. It is the first cause which unifies reality, the most positive and real element in our experience, and not the most indeterminate and passive.

There are two slightly different ways of arguing to the existence of an infinite and absolutely perfect thing. For that which is the ultimate source of everything is absolutely perfect because it is wholly active and in no way passive. The very meaning of source or cause implies that it acts upon other things, and is not itself acted upon. But that which is purely active is absolutely perfect because it has fulfilled its purpose and realized all its powers. There can be nothing incomplete in it since it is not passive in any way; everything in it is active and fulfilled. Moreover, since it is purely active, it is unlimited, because there is nothing in it to limit its activity, nothing other than activity. It is perfect and infinite.

It seems worth adding that these ways of arguing to God are basically the same as the five ways of St Thomas, for all arguments to God are surely basically the same. They are all different ways which aim at bringing home to the mind that reflection on the things around us makes us recognize the presence of the infinite. It is always a question of showing that, when we think of finite things, we are aware, by applying to them such ideas as that of cause, activity, good, and so on, of that which is perfect and infinite in the background of our thought. The limited things in the foreground do not fill up the whole content of our awareness. In short, it is always a question of showing that, if we make our thoughts explicit, we find we are aware of the infinite.

## IMPLICATIONS

Now, if this is so, what kind of knowledge do we have of the infinite first cause; what can we say about it? It is plainly necessary that we should answer this question if we are to discuss the problems that arise over God's providence. In the first place, there can be no doubt that our knowledge is indirect and obscure, because admittedly we are only aware of the infinite in the background of our consciousness. However, there are certain statements that can be made. We can say that it has no imperfection or limitation, and therefore can deny of it all the imperfections and limitations we find in the things around us. Hence it must be a simple unity without any division into parts. The reason is that, if a thing has parts, one part is not another part, and a whole made up of limited parts is not absolutely unlimited: each part is a restricted centre of activity, limited because not fully united with other parts. An infinite thing is such that we cannot use the word "not" about it in any sense of restriction or exclusion. If a thing has parts we can use the word "not" about it in this sense. If there are parts, the whole is not identical with the parts, or else we could not speak of parts. If the whole were identical with the parts, then the parts would be identical with one another, and there could be no parts. Consequently, an absolutely infinite thing must be a simple, undivided, whole.

It follows that an absolutely infinite thing is not extended in space, since extension involves parts, or at least the possibility of parts. Nor is it in time, since this, too, implies division. Time is made up of moments or phases which are distinct from one another and are, therefore, limited, one not being another. A thing in time is not a simple whole from every point of view.

It may, however, be asked whether time is really a limitation. Would a man really wish to have the past again? When he appears to have this wish, is it any more than a wish to enjoy in the future experiences similar to those of the past? The reply may be made that, even if this is true, it does not show that subjection to time is no limitation. The desires which a man has may be limited desires, and if a life in time involves limitation, then desires which are satisfied by such a life are more limited than desires for a life not subject to time at all.

So we can say that God is free from limitation. We can go on to say that God possesses every perfection we can conceive of in an unlimited degree. To explain what is meant by this will take a little longer. As I have said, God can only be said to have all perfections if he is the source of them all. Finite perfections could not, as such, be raised to infinite perfection, and there can only be infinite perfection if it contains finite perfections as their cause. This, however, raises a problem. We can know something of God by thinking of finite perfections raised to an infinite degree. But as such they cannot be raised in this way; when we attempt to do this we leave the finite perfections behind, and think of their cause which is infinite. How, then, does this help us to have any knowledge of God? It can only help us if there is likeness of some kind between the finite effect and the infinite cause, based on the fact that every cause must possess what it gives to its effect, and that the total cause of the whole being of a thing must contain what it gives to this dependent thing.

But in what sense does the cause contain the perfection of its effect? It has been objected that an apple is round and coloured, while God is neither round nor coloured, that by these very characteristics of roundness and colour the apple differs from God (R. L. Patterson, *The Conception of God in the Philosophy of Aquinas*, p. 299). What reply can we make to this? Plainly the difficulty arises through taking likeness to mean likeness of the direct kind with which we are familiar, for instance, between two blades of grass. But no defender of theism would suppose that likeness of this kind can exist between finite and infinite, and in so far as the objection is denying likeness of this kind it is pushing at an open door.

The obvious rejoinder is: what other kind of likeness can there be? Can there be any sense at all in which the creature is like the creator? To this I should reply: the sense in which the effect is like its total cause. This relationship of effect to total cause involves a unique kind of likeness. The first cause, though absolutely simple and in no way directly like its effects, yet contains in itself the power to produce them. The perfections of the effects are present in the cause in that way in which the power to create them is present. The effect is like its cause, because the cause contains what it gives, but it is a unique kind of likeness since what is given is contained in the cause in a unique way, namely, in its creative power.

Nevertheless, this leads to another difficulty. If this is true, how can the effect be, as it certainly is, in some sense unlike its cause? How can there be any element in the effect which is unlike the cause, since it would seem that like can only come from like? The effect is distinct from the cause and, therefore, the creature must in some sense be unlike the creator, but how can creatures be other than the creator? They are created out of no preexisting material which can explain it.

Surely the answer is that the creature is unlike the creator in so far as it is a limited kind of thing, and that it is limited for the very reason that it is a creature. Limitation is a lack of being or activity and as such is merely negative, but it is caused by that drawing away from the infinite which is involved in being derived from it. Limitation of causal activity is inherent in the very fact of causality, and it is meaningless to speak of the infinite cause producing an infinite effect. Hence, although in a sense like only comes from like, and although there is no preexisting material on which the first cause acts, yet the creature cannot be wholly like the creator. From one point of view the creature must necessarily be unlike the creator: likeness is not identity, and always implies some unlikeness. The creature is positive and real, and in this sense is like God; it is negative and limited because it is in the dependent order of being, and in this sense is unlike God.

To sum up, in our present experience we certainly do not know God in a fully adequate manner. How, then, do we know him? He is present to us as our cause, and hence in becoming aware of ourselves we become aware of God in so far as he is our cause. God is in this sense both immanent and transcendent. The knowledge is, of course, obscure, and it is only by reflection and analysis that we can make it explicit. How can we express this obscure knowledge that we have of God as our cause? We can use the word, God, which indicates the infinite cause as known to us, without referring particularly to anything we can say about him. Then we can use finite perfections to express God because he possesses them as their cause: we can say, for example, that God is a person. Finite perfections are true, but immeasurably inadequate, to express God. We can call God a person because, although he is infinitely beyond what we experience as personality, yet this is the highest perfection we know directly, and is contained in God's infinite perfection. All created perfections, the least as well as the greatest, are in one sense on an equal footing to express the infinite; the first cause contains them all, while all are inadequate. But the higher perfections have this advantage, that they are not lower than ourselves, and therefore convey the meaning to us better. Thus finite perfections are true, yet inadequate, to express God. The reason why they are not simply false is because creatures are dependent beings and not mere nothingness. Their perfections are real, but of a different order from that of infinite perfection, because there is nothing common to both in precisely the same sense.

Hence we can use the same words of God and creatures but, when we do so, we use them partly in the same and partly in a different sense. The creature is mighty and God is mighty, but God is mighty in the sense that, as cause, he contains the creature's perfection, and thus partly in a different sense. All agree that we use the same words analogically of God and creatures, but this, I submit, is the best explanation of analogy: it is based on the unique kind of likeness between cause and effect. This explanation is quite straightforward with regard to words like person or mighty, but it is a little more complex with regard to words like being, one, good, active. These involve in their very notion a reference to the first cause; being implies absolute being, one the absolutely simple, active pure activity, because in themselves being excludes not-being, one excludes division, activity excludes inactivity. The principle, however, is the same. They apply both to the finite and to the infinite, but in partly different senses: creatures have being, and God has being as their cause; creatures are one imperfectly and God perfectly; creatures are active but not wholly active, while God is purely active.

It amounts to this: the creature reveals the creator, though in an imperfect way, and hence we can know the creator through the creature, and can express the creator by using terms which refer primarily to the creature. These are true but inadequate when applied to the creator.

# CHAPTER III

# GOD'S LOVE AND

# PROVIDENCE

To discuss God's providence we must first discuss God's love, because his love determines his providential direction of creatures. Love depends on knowledge and will, because it means desire for an object, and therefore we must consider God's knowledge of men.

### THE MEANING OF GOD'S KNOWLEDGE

This at once raises a difficult problem. How can the infinite be aware of finite things, without the awareness of finite things involving limitation in himself? This is one of the chief objections raised against the Thomist system in the book I have already mentioned, *The Conception of God in the Philosophy of Aquinas*. The criticism is summed up on p. 296: ". . . we have been assured that a perfect knowledge of the divine essence involves, not only a general, but also a proper knowledge of all other things. But how can this be true if God be but a simple and absolute unity, a totally undifferentiated monad?"

I am not attempting to defend the Thomist system in every respect, but this objection may be thought to apply to any theory which holds that God is the infinite first cause. What, then, are we to say?

Now, although in one sense there is no limit to the possible scope of our knowledge, yet with us knowledge is a limited kind of activity. For, it is only one among other kinds of activity, and it is a process involving succession. Moreover we only have an obscure, not a comprehensive, knowledge of the infinite. This brings us to the point that must be stressed. God cannot possess knowledge as we possess it, for, if he is absolutely simple, he cannot possess any power or faculty which is not identical with his simple, infinite, perfection. It is true that, being the first cause, he possesses in himself, in the sense already explained, all the perfections of his creatures, and consequently in this sense possesses knowledge. Yet he only possesses it in this special way, and there is no direct likeness between our knowledge and God's simple perfection.

Cannot we say that God possesses knowledge, but not our kind of knowledge, that he possesses a knowledge free from all imperfection? No doubt there is a sense in which this is true, but certainly there is also a sense in which it is false, and we must be careful to distinguish between them. A knowledge freed from all limitation would be nothing else than the simple perfection of the infinite first cause. It would, therefore, only be knowledge in the same sense in which every created perfection is possessed by God. There can be no perfection possessed in a directly similar way by both creatures and creator, because there can be no direct likeness between them. Hence the true sense in which God can be said to possess knowledge is the same as that in which he can be said to possess all finite perfections, namely, as possessing that which he gives. The false sense is that which would imply an element in knowledge capable of being stripped of limitation, and then existing in God in a way directly similar to that in which it exists in creatures.

But, if this is so, the objection that God, if he is simple and undivided, cannot know limited and particular things, surely falls to the ground. God does not know in exactly the same way as we know. The problem of God's knowledge of creatures is no special problem; it is only a special aspect of the problem of reconciling finite with infinite. Finite and infinite are reconciled, I am suggesting, if we remember the relationship between them of effect to cause. The finite perfections of creatures imply no contradiction to the infinite perfection of God, because creatures are entirely derived from God and can add nothing to him: it is meaningless to speak of summing them together. Consequently, if finite adds nothing to infinite, knowledge of the finite adds nothing to knowledge of the infinite, and does not contradict it. In further explanation I can only repeat that God's knowledge is not like our knowledge, but is identical with his simple, infinite, perfection. I suggest, therefore, that this difficulty about God's knowledge is less formidable than has sometimes been supposed.

And here we should notice a point which is very important in connection with God's providence. If God's simple perfection includes knowledge in the sense explained, and if in God there is no time or succession but only the eternal present, then there is no contradiction in saying that God sees past and future events all together as present. There is nothing past or future to God, although he sees events in creation as past or future in relation to other events. Granted that the argument has been sound at an earlier stage, there seems no special difficulty about God's knowledge of future events. Of course future events which depend on the creature's free choice present a special problem, but that is rather the problem of free choice and God's causality than of God's knowledge of future events.

### THE MEANING OF GOD'S WILL

Next let us turn to the question of God's will. If what has just been said about God's knowledge is acceptable, we have only to apply the same line of reasoning to discussion of his will. Just as human knowledge is a limited power, so too is human will. It is limited because it is not identical with other powers which men possess, because it acts under the limitations of time, and because its scope is in certain respects limited. Therefore it follows, for reasons similar to those mentioned in connection with knowledge, that God does not have will as we have it. Will is included in his simple perfection only in the sense that he is able to create finite wills. We should bear this point in mind when faced with the problems which arise with regard to God's will.

One such problem is God's motive for creation. Why does God create? What is it which he desires when he creates, and how can creation satisfy his desire? Is he not entirely self-sufficient, and are not all his desires fully satisfied from eternity?

At once we come up against the inadequacy of our power to understand or express the infinite. It is true that God is absolutely self-sufficient, and needs nothing for his satisfaction. But we can express God, however imperfectly, in terms of finite activity, and therefore can say that he has a motive for creation. We speak analogically, and what we say is true only in the sense that the cause contains what it produces in its effects. God does not act from a motive in any sense that implies limitation or imperfection, nor in any sense that implies dependence on an object outside himself. Only that which is positive in the assertion applies to God. In the end all we can say is this. We have seen reasons for saying that God has created, and that this involves no contradiction. The act of creation implies no loss, no effort, in God because his power is infinite; consequently it requires no motive in the sense of satisfaction of an unsatisfied desire, to explain it. God is the uncaused cause, and his act of creation has no cause or motive other than himself.

But does not this imply that God's act of creation is entirely selfish, and that he has no desire for the happiness of creatures? Is not this a very low conception of God?

We must remember that God and creatures are in different orders of being. While it is right for a creature to make God the ultimate end of his action, it would be wrong, indeed it would be inconceivable, that God should make the creature the ultimate end of his action. It is for the good of creatures that God should create them with the ultimate motive of fulfilling his own will; this is the true order of things, on which the creature's happiness depends. If God acted unselfishly, in the sense of making the good of the creature the final end of his action, he would not in fact be acting unselfishly, since this would not be for the good of the creature. God acts for the good of the creature only by making the achievement of his own will the final end of his action.

Of course this does not mean that God has no desire for the good of the creature, only that this is not the final end. God wills the happiness of the creature, but wills it from the ultimate motive of fulfilling his own will. But, again, this does not mean that he only wills the happiness of the creature in order to gain something for himself: he is himself eternally and utterly happy. St Thomas says (*Summa Theol.* Ia, Qu. 44, art. 4, ad 1): "to act as a result of need only applies to an imperfect agent, when it is such as to be an agent and a patient. This is not true of God. Therefore he alone is supremely generous, because he does not act for his own advantage, but only through his goodness."

It may be asked: If God does not bring creatures into being in order to satisfy any need of his own, yet does so ultimately for no other reason than that he wills it, is not his action random and motiveless and without any reason? We cannot, however, conclude that God's action is random and motiveless because no desire, previously unsatisfied, is satisfied by the act of creation. The supreme reason for everything must be the fact that God wills it, for he is the infinite first cause. There is no cause or motive beyond God which can give value to any act. It is true that God has no desire which is unfulfilled before it is fulfilled, since he is perfect from eternity. Yet this does not mean that his action is motiveless: its motive is there, but, so far as God is concerned, the motive has done its work from eternity. As with every statement about God this, though true, is inadequate to express the whole truth. Creatures add nothing to God, and give him no additional satisfaction. Yet there are the best of reasons for the creation of creatures, namely, God's will on the one hand, and the happiness of the creatures on the other, which is what God wills.

## GOD'S FREEDOM AND NECESSITY

A discussion of God's will raises the question of God's freedom and necessity. Does he act freely or of necessity? The Church declares that God's act of creation is free and is not necessary, on the ground that, if it were necessary, the creature's existence would be necessary, and thus that the creature would not be a creature: pantheism would be implied.

But this raises the obvious question: How can God's act of creation be free, if God is absolutely simple and eternal, with no before or after in his action? Does not free choice imply that there was a time before the choice was made, and when the issue was still undecided? How can this be true of God? Moreover, it may be felt that, if God's freedom is difficult to understand, his necessity is no less so. If God is subject to necessity, does not this mean that there is a cause beyond the first cause, which determines the first cause? How can there be any principle which imposes necessity on God, and in view of which we are able to say that God could not do otherwise?

According to St Thomas a thing is necessary if it cannot not be (*Summa Theol.* Ia, Qu. 82, art. 1), that is to say, if its non-existence is inconceivable. Now, if this is so, there is a certain necessity about everything for, once a thing exists, there is a sense in which it could not exist. To understand what this sense is we must make a distinction between conditional and absolute necessity. There is conditional necessity if the necessity of one thing depends upon that of another, while there is absolute necessity if a thing cannot not exist in any circumstances whatever. Only the infinite first cause can be absolutely necessary, while creatures are necessary only in a conditional sense. If creatures exist they cannot not exist, but there is nothing in themselves which causes this condition to be fulfilled; it is only fulfilled because God wills it. On the other hand, while the existence of the creature is only conditionally necessary, the possibility of its existence is absolutely necessary. If a thing exists nothing can alter, or ever could have altered, the possibility of its existence. The reason for this is that God necessarily exists, and necessarily has the power to create what in fact he does create.

Everything, then, which exists is necessary in some sense, and, indeed, necessity is involved in the very idea of existence or being or activity. Necessity simply emphasizes that aspect of being or activity, from which being or activity can be regarded as incapable of not-being or inactivity. But, just as we can distinguish between the absolute being or activity of God and the dependent being or activity of creatures, so too we can distinguish between the absolute necessity of God and the conditional necessity of creatures. Just as we cannot think of a finite thing without thinking of the infinite cause in the background, so too we cannot think of conditional necessity without thinking also of absolute necessity.

How, then, are we to deal with the problem of God's necessity? Plainly God's existence is absolutely necessary, because it is impossible that he should not exist, and the impossibility is quite unconditional. But does this imply that there is some power beyond God to which he is subject, and which enforces his existence? Equally plainly this is not so, since there is nothing more ultimate than God. When we speak of God's necessity we refer to a necessity which is derived from God himself, or rather, which is identical with God himself. Every principle of reason and necessity must have its source in God, for there is no source beyond God. In this sense every such principle depends simply on God's will. We must, however, remember that we are using the word, will, of God analogically, and that in him it refers to something determined from eternity. Hence although these principles of reason and necessity in one sense depend simply on God's will, nevertheless they are eternally necessary, and could not conceivably be otherwise. What God wills he wills from eternity. God's own necessity is derived from himself, yet it is a necessity of the most absolute kind because it is imposed from eternity.

So much for the necessity of God's act, and now let us turn to its freedom. Although God's act is absolutely necessary yet it is free in the sense that it is entirely unimpeded. It is also free in the sense that it is not the result of any external cause, since God is the source of all causality. But is God's act of creation free in the sense of being the result of free choice? An act of choice implies that before the act took place there was a conflict of desire, more than one course being possible, and that the agent was not so determined either from outside or from within that only one course could be followed. Now no one suggests that God's action is ever free in the sense that, before he acts, he is in a state of indetermination and conflict of desire, and that he then makes a free choice and determines his action. God's action cannot be free in this sense, because it is determined from eternity, and has no before or after. Yet God's act of creation may be called in a certain sense an act of free choice.

For, though it is an act which is determined from eternity by God, yet its term or effect is not, if we take the effect in itself, necessary in the absolute sense. There is no contradiction, if we speak of the created effect in itself, in saying that it might not have been brought about, or might have been different from what it is. God's act of creation is an act eternally determined, but it is an act the effect of which is only conditionally necessary, only necessary because God so determines it; looked at in itself, the effect might have been otherwise.

In the light of this let us look at the declaration on the subject made by the Vatican Council. It condemns anyone who "should say that God created, not by a will free from all necessity, but as necessarily as he necessarily loves himself"

(Denzinger, 1805). How can we explain this, seeing that there is only one simple act in God, and that this is determined from eternity? We can do so if, and only if, we explain exactly what we mean. Although God's act is absolutely simple we must distinguish between that effect of the act which consists in the maintenance of God's own being, and that effect which consists in creation. We have to express God as if he were the effect of his own causality, inadequate though this mode of expression is. Now God's act, so far as it results in the first of these effects, results in something which could not be otherwise, while his act, so far as it results in the second effect, results in something which, taken in itself, might be otherwise. Hence, bearing in mind this distinction we can see a sense in which God's act of creation can be called freely chosen, because there is no necessity about the creature considered in itself. On the other hand God's love of himself is not free in this sense. Of course God's love of himself is free in the sense that God is the first cause, and his act of love is entirely self-determined and entirely unimpeded. It is necessary, however, in the sense that it is determined from eternity, and that God could not conceivably fail to love himself, because this love must necessarily exist.

Thus there is no contradiction in the Council's words, if we remember, as we must remember throughout, the limitations under which we labour in our attempts to express the infinite, and if we remember, too, the different senses in which both freedom and necessity can be used. The object of the Council's decree is clearly to insist on the fact that creatures are wholly dependent on the creator, and to prevent any suggestion of pantheism, which would be implied by a denial of this dependence.

So far in this chapter I have been discussing what is meant by God's knowledge and will, and have been examining certain questions which arise in this connection. This has prepared the way for considering God's love of his creatures, which is the central theme of the chapter owing to its importance for considering his providence. I have been speaking of God's knowledge and will, because love depends on knowledge and will in our own experience, and we can only express God's activity by applying to him those kinds of activity which we find in ourselves.

## GOD'S LOVE FOR CREATURES

Now all perfection consists in unity, since the absence of unity implies division and division implies limitation. All perfection consists in freedom from limitation, which is brought about by unity. All perfection consists in the realization of a thing's powers, and the realization of a thing's powers consists in the gaining of the object which it seeks, in unity with this object. Hence all perfection consists in the satisfaction of desire. True perfection consists in the satisfaction of right desires, which are right because they lead to ultimate satisfaction and perfection. False perfection consists in the satisfaction of wrong desires, which are wrong because they lead to ultimate frustration of desire.

What, then, is love? In its most general sense love is desire or will to do good to someone or something known to us. For a thing is good in so far as it fulfils a given purpose, that is to say, given desires or powers. Hence a right love is desire to bring about the ultimate good of someone or something, while a wrong love is desire to bring about a good which is no true good because it only fulfils an immediate purpose, but not the ultimate purpose. What kind of love, then, is the most perfect kind? Clearly that kind which seeks for the most perfect end, and the most perfect end is that which removes limitation over the widest possible field, which means the most complete kind of unity for the greatest possible number of beings. We need not consider beings which are not conscious persons, so the question is what is the closest kind of unity between conscious persons. The answer surely is that this kind of unity consists in complete harmony of desire, based on clear knowledge of one another. Hence we reach the conclusion that unselfish love is the highest kind of love, because it means the making of another person's good the end or motive of action, the harmonizing of one person's desires with those of another.

It may be worth while to call to mind how the normal scale of values accepted by man, the kind of conduct which is normally regarded as admirable, bears this out. A man is not admired if he looks after his own interests, but he is admired if he looks after the interests of someone else for no personal gain, though the other person, taken as a unit, is no more valuable than himself. It seems, then, that what is regarded as valuable is unity among human beings, arising from knowledge of one another and will for one another's good. It is not merely that human life cannot go on unless men serve one another, but we recognize that it is good that this should be so. We recognize that a society in which each member got for himself all that he needed, and did nothing for others, would not be the kind of society we should admire. The value of unselfish conduct is not derived solely from the fact that the need of another man, considered as another unit, is satisfied. Of course it is right that individual needs should be satisfied, but the ideal goes beyond this. If two lives are of equal value, and if one man is in danger and can only be saved at the risk of another man's life, we should admire the man who would risk himself. What we admire seems to be the union or harmony of will between two people, and the readiness of an individual to foster this union, even at the risk of suffering.

Now what of God's love in himself? If we take love in its most general sense as the desire for someone's good, then clearly we can say that God loves himself, and indeed that he is love. For, I must repeat, we have to express God as though he first sought for his own good and then attained it, although we know we are trying to express that which goes beyond this —that God's goodness or purpose is fully achieved from eternity. We can say, therefore, that God loves his own perfection, and that this love is perfectly and eternally satisfied. We can further identify God with love, and say that he is love, because he is absolutely simple, and in him the subject who loves, the object who is loved, and the love itself are all identical.

There is no special difficulty about this, but it raises the further question: Is that all we can say about God's love in himself? Is it only the desire for his own good? If God's infinite perfection implies no unselfish love, how can unselfish love be the high ideal it is for his creatures?

Without the Christian revelation it would not be easy to answer this. We cannot say that God loves creatures with an unselfish love, if this is taken to mean that he makes them the ultimate object of his act of creation. I have already explained this, and shown the sense in which he creates for the good of the creature. But in any case Christianity gives us the answer through the doctrine of the Trinity, three Persons in one Godhead. Through this doctrine we are taught that unselfish love lies at the very centre and source of reality. By the unselfish love in the Trinity God is the source of unselfish love in creatures, though creatures, being creatures, possess the perfection in a different way.

This must suffice to give some idea of God's love in himself, and we can go on to consider rather more fully his love for creatures. Of his very nature God can only desire the good of creatures, for anything else would be meaningless. The ultimate purpose of God's act of creation is simply the fulfilment of his will, as I have said, but the perfection and happiness of creatures is the object which he wills. Such is God's goodness, or perfection of activity, that not only does he will his own happiness, but also the happiness of creatures as a kind of overflow of goodness. There can be no doubt that God loves creatures, in the sense of willing their good, for this is involved in the very idea of creation. Creation means the carrying out of a plan or purpose, and this purpose is nothing else than the realization of the powers given to creatures.

Now, when God loves creatures, what is it that he wills to do for them? He wills of course to perfect the powers he has given them, but what is the object towards which these powers tend? Since perfection is union, what God wills to achieve is union of the creature with himself, or in other words, the love of the creature for himself. God loves the creature, and desires the creature's love, for only in that way can he gain what he loves.

Here another difficulty will be felt. Is not God entirely satisfied by his own perfection, and how can he have any desire for the creature's good? This can be answered by saying that, although the creature's good can cause God no further satisfaction, yet God can act for the creature's good. But then the question comes: If this is so, how can there be that complete harmony between creatures and creator, which is required for perfect union? On the creature's side how can there be unselfish love for God, if there is no further good that the creature can wish him?

## CREATURES' LOVE FOR GOD

We must distinguish once more between God's essential good which is necessarily achieved, and the good of his creatures which he wills, though it adds nothing to his happiness, and which is not necessarily achieved. Creatures can love God in the sense of willing his essential good, only by harmonizing their own wills with the will of God, and making God's will the determining cause of their own wills. Even though God's essential purpose is eternally achieved (so that to speak of a purpose in God is utterly inadequate), the creature is able to accept this for himself, or not to do so. By acceptance he practises unselfish love of God. Now the creature expresses his acceptance of God's will by acting in accordance with it. Thus, although there is a clear distinction between God's own essential good and the good he wills for creatures, yet the creature's unselfish love of God can only be shown by his efforts to carry out what God wills for creatures. We reach the conclusion, therefore, that it is only by aiming at his own perfection and happiness, and that of his fellow creatures, that the creature can show his love of God. At the same time he can love God unselfishly, because he can make God's will the final reason and motive for doing this.

However, the question is by no means covered by what has been said. There remains the difficulty that union based on such love as this, when God is unaffected in himself by what happens to the creature, seems a very imperfect union. We have experience of much closer union in human affairs. Two men may be agreed upon a course of action, but they may or may not have one another's interests at heart, and be in full sympathy with one another. There is all the difference between a business agreement among strangers and the kind of understanding that may exist among friends. The love between creatures and creator, as I have described it, may seem far short of that which is possible between human beings. But can we say more; can God fully sympathize with creatures, rejoice in their joy, and grieve in their sorrow?

There are two questions here: first, is such a union as this with God necessary for the highest happiness of creatures, and, secondly, can we explain the difficulties which are involved, if we think such a union is necessary?

It is important to say a few words about the first question. It is the teaching of the Church that men can never, without supernatural grace, enjoy that intimate union with God which is called the beatific vision—that man's natural powers alone are insufficient for this. Hence we cannot say that the closest kind of union with God is necessary for the perfection of man's natural powers alone; we can only say that it is necessary when supernatural powers have also been given. So the question we have to ask is: How can there be, even in the beatific vision, that close union between creature and creator which may exist between creatures and, further, how can God have any union of sympathy with men during their life on earth? How can God love men in such a way as to sympathize with their joys and sorrows, when he can never suffer any sorrow himself or have any more joy than he already has? We can understand, it may be thought, so far as we can understand the things of God at all, how he can love creatures in the sense of willing their perfection and happiness, but how can there be that closer union between creature and creator, in which each would reflect the experience of the other? Can we apply to God in any true sense the sorrow and joy of the father of the prodigal son? How can there be joy in heaven over the penitent sinner?

It will be best to separate the two sides of the question, and ask, first of all, how the happiness of the creature can be a happiness to God, before we ask how God can sympathize with the creature's sorrow. It should be noticed that the question is concerned with God in his own essence; in his human nature, that is to say, in Christ, God can of course sympathize with man's experience, and no difficulty arises.

So the question deals with God in his own essence. To discuss it I must refer to what was said about the likeness of the creature to God. Creatures are wholly derived from God, and therefore God's simple perfection contains the finite perfections of creatures, though in a sense we cannot fully grasp. Since this is so, and since God rejoices in his own perfection (though the word, rejoice, or its equivalent, is of course only true analogically of God), it follows that God rejoices in every created perfection, because this is in a certain sense a likeness and revelation of himself. There cannot, needless to say, be any real difference in God between the joy he has in himself and the joy he has in creatures, because he is absolutely one and undivided. Yet there are two points, it seems to me, which we ought to bear in mind.

First, we should notice this. When one thing is derived from another, and is like the other thing, it derives what beauty it possesses from that of which it is a likeness, and the satisfaction found in its beauty is really found in the source of its beauty. Undoubtedly there is much that is mysterious in the idea of the creature as a likeness of God but, granting that the creature is like God, the problem of God's joy in his creatures does not present, I think, any contradiction: there is meaning in saying that God takes joy in the perfection and happiness of creatures because they are a reflection of his own perfection and happiness.

Secondly, we must take into account the obscurity of our knowledge of God, real though it is. Even knowledge and will, as I have argued, can only be said to exist in God in the sense that he includes in himself all that is derived from him. The same is true of his joy. Creatures exist, but they add nothing to God, because they are entirely derived from him, and God's knowledge of them adds nothing to God for the same reason. But, if this is so, God can rejoice in his creatures, and this can add nothing to his essential joy. All the same it should be noticed that this does not in any way imply pantheism. Creatures are images of God because they are the effects of his causality, but an effect is distinct from its cause.

This still leaves us with the question: How can God share in his creature's sorrows? Sufferings as such are evils, even though not moral evils, because they are the consciousness of frustration of some kind. Although God cannot suffer in himself, undoubtedly he is aware (in the sense in which we can use the word about God) of the sufferings of creatures, because all creation is caused and planned by him.

This at once brings up the profound and baffling problem: how can God be aware of evil in creation, and yet suffer nothing in himself? Some light is thrown on this problem if we bear in mind that God sees all things from eternity, and looks at the whole process of created activity from the point of view of the end, which at length is reached. If the creature in the end attains supreme happiness, the sufferings endured in the passage through time are nothing in comparison. If these sufferings have not been the creature's own fault, he will recognize, when they are over, that it was well worth while to endure them in order to reach the goal. If they have been due to the creature's fault, he will recognize that he was himself to blame, and that the punishment was a small thing in comparison with the

happiness finally gained. In any case from the standpoint of
eternity temporal sufferings must appear in a very different
light from that in which they appear now.

Can we, however, go further than this? To be aware of the
creature's sufferings, and even to understand them fully from
the standpoint of eternity, is not the same as to sympathize
with them, for this implies an experience of the sufferings like
that of the sufferer himself. Can God sympathize in the full
sense with the creature's sufferings, while he suffers?

In the full sense of sympathy it seems clearly impossible that
God in his own essence should sympathize with the sufferings
of creatures; he cannot share them, if he is eternally happy.
But there are certain points to bear in mind, even when this is
said.

We have always to remember that, if God could share in
the sufferings of creatures in the sense of suffering in his own
essence, there would be no God, and hence there would be no
final happiness which the creature could ultimately enjoy. We
should have taken away from the creature the hope, which
alone can explain and relieve his suffering.

Then, although God cannot in his own essence suffer with
us, yet he is aware of our sufferings, and therefore can help us.
We may perhaps use the comparison of a journey to represent
the creature's relation to God before the end is reached. During
the passage through time in the process of perfection we are on
the journey, and God is only to be found at the end.  God cannot himself come to meet us while we are still on the journey,
and yet it is only by meeting us that he could fully share in
our sufferings. We can only meet him face to face in absolute
happiness, when the journey is finished.

What, then, we can say about the love of sympathy and
friendship between creatures and creator amounts to this.
There can be a sharing in happiness, because the creature can
share in God's happiness, while God can rejoice in an image
of himself. There can be communication of a gift from one to
the other, which St Thomas says is essential to friendship, in

so far as God communicates his own presence and beatitude to the creature, while the creature gives back the image of this beatitude, which is seen in himself. There cannot be a sharing of suffering between the creature and God in his own essence, but suffering belongs to the time before the love between creature and creator has come to its full fruition.

I may sum up by putting the question in the form: How can there be close union of love between creatures and God, when it makes no difference to God whether the creature is happy or unhappy? It is true, we can reply, that the creature is in no way necessary for God's happiness. Nevertheless, the happiness of the creature can be a happiness to God in so far as the creature is an image of God, and hence a reflection of that which causes happiness to God, namely, his own infinite perfection. When it is said that it makes no difference to God whether the creature is happy or unhappy, we must bear in mind that (except through the creature's own fault) sorrow is passing, and in the end happiness alone remains, which can be shared with God. While it is true that the creature's sufferings make no difference to God, it is also true that in the end they make no difference to the creature himself. Hence in the end they form no barrier to sympathy between the creature and God.

So in this chapter I have tried to show that God knows and loves his creatures, and to show in what sense this is true. It is not difficult to apply the conclusions to God's providential government of creation. God created for a purpose, and the purpose was the perfection of creatures, and he had a plan for bringing this about, which followed from the natures the creatures were given. God's providence, therefore, consists in his direction of creation towards the end it is designed for, and, since God is almighty and all-good, we might suppose there was nothing more to be said. But here we come up against the hard fact of evil.

CHAPTER IV

# EVIL

The conclusions reached in the last chapter suggest a very different state of things from that which we actually find in the world. God wills, I have said, that creatures should be united with him, that the powers he has given them should be realized, and that their purpose (which is his purpose) should be fulfilled. We might expect, therefore, that the perfection of creatures would be carried forward smoothly and steadily to its completion without any frustration or delay at any stage. In fact we are faced with a very different situation. We find around us natural powers frustrated and perverted, and ends sought which lead away from the true purpose of life. We find diseases and calamities, and crimes committed in defiance of God's will. In short we find God's plan for creation apparently in large measure a failure, and often discord and disunion between the aims of creature and those of the creator, instead of harmony and union.

## HOW CAN EVIL BE COMPATIBLE WITH GOD'S PROVIDENCE?

Thus we must now consider the problem of reconciling the loving providence of God, who is almighty and all-good, with the presence of evil in creation. At first sight it looks as though there were a direct and inevitable contradiction: if God is almighty and only wills the happiness of the creature, how can there be any conceivable explanation of evil?

Among those who believe in God some may be inclined to say that evil is a mystery which we cannot, and need not attempt to, fathom—that God's purposes are beyond our comprehension, that evil is mainly due to sin, and that sin, though undoubtedly raising a most profound problem, raises a problem rooted in the infinite, too deep for our understanding.

We must not, however, appeal to mystery, and give no further answer. There appears to be a contradiction; we seem to be making two incompatible statements, namely, that God wills the good of creatures, and yet that creatures suffer evil, or, that God is the cause of all things, and yet that creatures act in opposition to God. We can be rightly challenged to explain what is meant by statements we make.

A mystery in the theological sense is a truth taught by the Church which we only know through revelation, and which, even when revealed, we cannot fully understand—the Trinity or the Incarnation, for example. We can understand something of what is taught, but we realize that our grasp is very imperfect. The point which is important here is this. In so far as we can make true statements about a mystery, they cannot conflict with other true statements. We cannot appeal to mystery to make sense of a contradiction. We cannot say that God is almighty and wills the good of a creature, and yet that the creature's good is not realized, or that a man determines his own choice and yet that he is wholly determined by God, and, when challenged to explain, merely reply that it is a mystery. We must show that the statements do not conflict when rightly understood, or else we must modify one of them in some way. Hence we cannot solve this problem of evil simply by saying that God's purposes are beyond our comprehension, or that evil is due to sin, but that it is a mystery how a creature can misuse his free will, when God is almighty and all-good.

We must try, then, to give a reasoned answer to this problem. As a first step let us ask what precisely is meant by evil, for otherwise the nature of the problem will not be clear.

## THE MEANING OF EVIL

Evil is the opposite of good, and by calling a thing good we mean that it fulfils its purpose: a knife is good if it fulfils its purpose of cutting. A thing, therefore, is evil in so far as it fails to fulfil its purpose.

The question may be asked: How is this true of a knife? Surely, if it does not cut well, it has no power to cut, and does not this mean that it has no purpose to cut? Certainly, I should reply, a blunt knife has no power to cut, but yet men have the power to make sharp knives. The purpose of a tool depends upon the purpose of its maker; the purpose of a living thing resides more completely in itself, since it has the power in itself, if not hindered, to realize its natural purpose. Therefore, both a knife and, say, a tree can be called evil in so far as they fail to realize their purposes, the purpose of the knife being that of its maker, the purpose of the tree being that of its natural powers.

Now, if this is the meaning of good and evil, it follows that evil as such, evil in itself, is negative: a thing is evil so far as it fails to fulfil its purpose, to realize its powers. Evil, therefore, does not imply in itself anything positive, but only a not-acting, the absence or privation of some perfection due to a thing's nature or purpose. If a knife is blunt, this means that it does not realize the purpose of a knife, which is that of a tool for cutting; if a tree is stunted, this means that the powers of the tree have not been realized.

Nevertheless it will be felt that such an explanation cannot be the whole truth about evil. Pain is evil, and surely pain is very positive? And is not a sinful act a positive evil, seeing that it produces so much harm?

This difficulty is, I think, largely due to a misunderstanding. I am not saying that an evil *thing* is merely negative, but only that evil in itself, as such, is negative. Plainly, if evil means the failure to realize a purpose, to possess a perfection which is due, it can never exist by itself; since it is negative the term, evil, can only refer to the limitations of a positive thing. It follows, therefore, that, although evil itself is negative, the evil thing in which evil is present is positive, though not so positive as it ought to be.

Hence to speak of evil as such is apt to be misleading, though it is difficult to avoid using the phrase. We cannot really take evil apart from good, if evil means the absence of a good which a thing ought to possess. We can only take evil apart from good in the sense that we can think of a thing with certain powers realized, and also with these powers unrealized, thereby seeing the difference between its two states, and seeing what it lacks when it is evil.

Why, then, do we find that there is something positive about, for example, bodily pain? I should answer in this way. Pain is the awareness of a positive thing, in this case, the body which, though partly fulfilling its natural purpose, is partly frustrated. The body is painful because its natural processes are frustrated in some degree: pain is the consciousness of frustrated life. But life cannot be wholly frustrated, since, if it were, no life would remain. It is the living, positive, thing which, owing to its frustration, is painful: what from one aspect is good is from another aspect and on the whole evil, because it seeks a further good which it needs and cannot get.

We may put it in this way. Although evil as such is negative, yet the evil thing, being deprived of the good which is natural to it, is affected by the evil. A living body, where activity is frustrated through the lack of some perfection due to it, tends to have the whole purpose of its remaining activity impaired, and, instead of healthy life, increasing frustration tends to result. A living thing is dynamic, and its activity, which naturally tends towards its preservation, may, if lacking some necessary perfection, now work towards its corruption. Once a thing is defective it may tend to become more and more defective, until it dies. The evil consists in a lack of the good due to it, but the evil thing tends as a result to lose further good, and the consciousness of this process is pain. The good tendencies strive to fight against the corruption, but they are too weak, and it is painful to feel their disorder and frustration. When a living thing lacks something which its nature requires, it suffers from a want, an unsatisfied desire or tendency, not a mere lack, but frustration. In short, though evil is negative, an evil thing is positive, but, since its efforts to preserve itself are frustrated, awareness of the positive thing is painful.

The same is true of the evil resulting from free choice, that is to say, sin. Sin is the choice of a wrong end in conduct, of an end which will not realize all a creature's powers, and will not make him ultimately happy. Sin is not merely the choice of a lesser good than is possible, but of a lesser good which in the particular circumstances conflicts with the greater good. Sin, therefore, as such is negative, but the sinner is positive, and his sin is positive in so far as it involves the choice of a positive good, though a positive good which conflicts with ultimate good. Sin is not merely imperfection, but it is perversion, because it is a choice which actually leads away from final perfection, towards disunion from God.

Take, for example, an act of cruelty. There is some perversion in a man's desires, and he gets satisfaction from inflicting pain on others. He deliberately chooses the satisfaction. The act is sinful because it produces in the victim pain, which is due to lack of some perfection, and because the will to do this leads in the criminal to lack of union with God, and therefore to his own limitation. But the sinful act is positive in so far as the doer of the act of cruelty gets some immediate satisfaction and performs a positive act, though it causes pain to the victim and ultimately pain to the doer himself.

These remarks on evil are very necessary if we are to see what solution can be found to the apparent contradiction between the presence of evil in creation and God's providence. We can at least conclude from what has been said that, since evil as such means the lack of a good which is needed, and since it has no positive meaning, there exists no positive principle of evil, independent of good. The problem is to explain, not any such rival principle, but how there can be a lack of the good naturally due to creatures, when God is almighty and wills that the powers and purpose of his creatures should be realized.

The next step, then, is to examine carefully what is meant by God's omnipotence and goodness in regard to creatures. Are these attributes of God really contradicted by the presence of evil in creation?

## THE MEANING OF GOD'S OMNIPOTENCE

Let us first take God's omnipotence. Manifestly it does not mean that God could make an infinitely perfect creature, for that which is perfect in every way and from every point of view is not a creature, but only God himself. A second God is contradictory. Nor does it mean that God could do anything else which is contradictory; he could not make a thing both square and round, or combine any other incompatible qualities in the same thing. A creature must be limited; he must be confined to his own particular nature, for instance as a human being, and cut off from all that is incompatible with this. Thus, when we speak of God as almighty, we do not mean that there is no limit to what he can do in the perfecting of his creatures. Every creature is limited, even though the limitations may be capable of progressive reduction to an indefinite extent.

It may be objected that to say this implies limitation in God, since it implies that he is subject to certain laws of contradiction, of what is possible and of what is not possible, which he cannot transgress. I have already touched on this subject when discussing whether God's acts are free or necessary, and it is important to apply here what I said before. Since God is the source of all things, and the source from eternity, we are bound (speaking in the inadequate way in which alone we can speak about God) to call his acts free because no cause can operate upon him, and yet necessary because everything in God exists from eternity and cannot be otherwise than it is.

Hence we must answer this question about the limits of

God's creative power in the following way. The laws of contradiction, which limit the possibilities of creation, cannot be laws to which God is subject as to a necessity logically previous to himself; if so he would not be God. Such laws must be entirely derived from God, yet they are necessary and unchangeable. To make a square circle is meaningless, and it is meaningless because the structure of reality makes it meaningless. The structure of reality depends on God who is uncaused, but it is settled from eternity and cannot, therefore, be other than it is. What is conceivable and what is inconceivable in creation is the result of God's nature, which is settled by God himself but from eternity, and hence what is conceivable and inconceivable, though dependent on God's will alone, is absolutely necessary.

It is no contradiction, then, to say that God's creative power is limited by the limitations which necessarily govern the perfections of the creature. But why, it will be asked, if this is so, do you call God almighty? What meaning is left to God's omnipotence, if God's power to create must necessarily be limited?

God is almighty in the sense that he has the power to create everything that is conceivable; in the sense that no power possible to him is either lacking or thwarted, and that the limit of the possible is the limit of the conceivable. Moreover God can gradually increase the perfection of a creature to an indefinite extent, though no creature can ever be so perfect that more perfection is inconceivable.

## THE MEANING OF GOD'S GOODNESS

Let us turn to God's goodness. God can do everything that is conceivable, but what limits are there to what God wills to do?

I have already given reasons for saying that God wills the good of creatures. Nevertheless, his will for the good of creatures must correspond with his creative power, and we have seen that there are limits to what this can do. Hence, in spite of

God's infinite goodness, there are limits to the good he wills for them, but these limits are only the limits of the possible. God's goodness to creatures is limited only in so far as the creature's power to benefit from God's goodness is limited.

On the other hand, apart from the limits of the possible imposed by the nature and circumstances of the creature, God's goodness must be unlimited. It seems quite inconceivable that God, for inscrutable reasons of his own, not connected with the limitations inherent in the creature, should ever will less good to the creature than it is capable of receiving. To say that God might do this is surely to deny his absolute perfection, since to do less good is less perfect than to do more good. Hence to say this is contradictory, for it is to say that God is not God, that his purpose to create is not his purpose.

It is important to avoid misunderstanding on this point. It can hardly be denied that God's perfecting of a creature must be limited by the creature's nature and circumstances; a man cannot receive the same perfection as an angel. But the question is: Does God always give the greatest amount of help which the creature, with its particular nature and circumstance can receive, or does he sometimes give less for no other reason than that he does not will to give more? The answer cannot be in doubt: God always gives the greatest help possible to ensure the perfection of a creature as quickly, completely, and securely as possible. There can be no inscrutable reasons which could make God fail to do this, because there can be no inscrutable reasons which could make God limit himself; the idea is contradictory. We may be sure, then, that God always gives the greatest help possible to a man in order to prevent him sinning, and to secure his salvation.

It is sometimes objected that to say this is to say that God is determined by his own creatures, which would of course be absurd. Such an objection, however, seems baseless. It is not a matter of God's being limited by his creatures, but only of his being unlimited by his own nature. God cannot limit himself in any way, because this would not be an act, but a failure to act. Consequently it seems clear that God must help the creature to the fullest extent possible, since to do otherwise would be to fail to act. By the very act of creation God reveals his purpose that the creature should be perfected; it is meaningless to suggest that he might change his purpose, or not fulfil it in the quickest and most effective way possible. It is contradictory, therefore, to say that God might, if he chose, show more love for any creature he has created than he does show.[1]

The conclusion, then, is that, although we can rightly call God almighty and infinitely good, nevertheless we do not thereby deny—indeed we imply—that there must be limits to the perfection which God can give to creatures. Now does this help us to explain the presence of evil?

## LIMITS TO THE PERFECTION WHICH GOD CAN GIVE TO CREATURES

I think it does, if we bear the following in mind. It is reasonable to suppose that everything created is designed to have a special kind of beauty and, if it has consciousness, a special kind of happiness. The nature of the beauty and happiness depend on the structure of the thing created, which may be— as in fact it is in the world in which we live—very complex. If it is complex the good of the whole may demand that some

---

[1] Hence I cannot agree with the following sentences in the article "Enfer" in the *Dictionnaire de théologie Catholique:* "To say that God owes salvation in the end to all is to impose upon him a necessity in the very realm of the gratuitous and to place limits on his creative love arising from the creature itself and the creature's sin. With more love for such creatures God would not have made hell; that would have been a degree of free and sovereign love which he has not willed." How can this be so if God is love, as we know he is? Lest it be thought that I have possibly misrepresented the author's thought in my translation the original French of the quotation is added here: "Dire que Dieu doit le salut final à tous, c'est mettre en lui une nécessité dans le domaine même du surabondant et c'est faire imposer des limites à son amour créateur par la créature même et par le péché de la créature. Avec plus d'amour pour telles créatures, Dieu n'aurait pas fait l'enfer; mais c'était un degré d'amour libre et indépendant et il ne l'a pas voulu." (*D.T.C.* vol. 5, 1, col. 117).

parts should suffer frustration for a time; certain temporary evils may be inevitable, if the particular kind of good, which this kind of creation alone can possess, is to reach its perfection. It may be far more valuable that this unique beauty and happiness should be realized than that no frustration should occur—a frustration which in any case is only passing. If temporary frustration is the unavoidable condition for final perfection, then God cannot avoid permitting the end if he is to bring about the good, even though he is almighty.

What I am saying is that the ultimate and highest good of the whole may require frustration for a time in the parts. I should like to try and explain this more carefully.

First, take the words "of the whole". Only God is absolutely simple; every creature must be complex to some degree, a one-in-many, as is the universe in which we find ourselves. Therefore it is in the very nature of a created thing that there should be the possibility of parts, and hence the possibility that the good of the whole may demand some sacrifice in the parts. In fact we can see that this is true in the world around us. There may be no need for a particular tree to die at a particular time, but, if trees never died, the process of nature could not go on, and the particular tree is part of the process. We realize, when we reflect, that, though a particular evil, taken by itself, may be avoidable, it may very well be unavoidable if we take the widest point of view.

Again, the kind of creation in which we, as human beings, find ourselves is social; it does not consist of a single person but of many persons who have a complex relationship to one another, and who can affect one another for good or for evil. Since God desires the good of his creatures, this social organization must be designed to produce a beauty and happiness arising from union and harmony among many individuals. Without the social structure which exists among mankind it is reasonable to suppose that this particular kind of beauty and happiness could not be produced, and it is presumably unique and has a unique value. We can see, however, that it carries with it the danger of a special kind of evil, if the individual acts wrongly. Since human beings are able to work for one another's happiness, they are also able to work for one another's harm: there is the possibility that the innocent may suffer. The possibility of the evil is bound up with the possibility of the good, and the one cannot exist without the other.

Then take the words, "the ultimate good". There are strong reasons, it seems to me, for holding that every creature, if it is to be perfected, must be built up gradually from imperfection to perfection, starting in imperfection and advancing through a process subject to time, or at least some kind of duration or succession. For the creature is of its very nature entirely dependent on God, possessing in itself no power to maintain its being. But, unless its life is in some sense a process, with a before and after, how can this be so? If there is no before and after in its life, if there is only an indivisible present, the creature could not conceivably come to an end and, if it could not come to an end, how could it be dependent on God? God alone can, in the strict sense, be eternal. It seems to follow necessarily that every creature must have a life subject to succession, while the highest kind of creature must also have the power to progress in perfection. God, being infinite, can create beings who are capable of further perfection without end, and, therefore, the highest kind of creature must be such that its perfection can continue to increase indefinitely.

Now, if this is so, the possibility of evil must be present to the creature, if it is capable of the greatest good. For the creature starts in imperfection, and this involves the possibility that it may fail to go forward to perfection: what is not yet perfect may conceivably not become perfect. This again makes it possible that frustration of the creature's powers and purpose may occur, and hence evil. If the creature is not yet perfect and has the power to choose its conduct, it may choose a course which does not lead to perfection.

Moreover, if the creature's life is successive, we can see that the evil it suffers may be passing, and the happiness it gains in the end may far outweigh the evil. The problem of reconciling evil with God's omnipotence is thus made easier. There need be no question of permanent evil but only of a passing evil at the earlier stages of the creature's progress to perfection, inevitable if perfection is to be reached, but of small consequence in comparison with the good ultimately to be gained.

Finally, take the words, "the highest good". If the thing created is a complex whole, it may contain parts of different value, but the purpose of the whole will be to realize the highest value it contains. This is the situation we find in the world around us. Man stands at the head of the visible creation, because, with his powers of mind and soul, there is no limit to the knowledge and perfection he may eventually acquire. Lesser things, capable of only a lesser perfection, seem designed to serve the purpose of men. Hence there are several considerations we must bear in mind, when we speak of the good of a creature. We must remember that we refer to the highest good of the creature, which alone is its true good. It may be inevitable that the lesser good, which ought to serve the purpose of the greater good, should be sacrificed. This may be the only way to realize the highest good which the particular thing as a whole can realize: it may be more valuable that the good in question should be realized than that there should be no frustration in the parts which are of lesser value. It may be better that the lives of plants and animals should be frustrated than that men should have no chance of existence.

## THE POSSIBILITY OF EVIL INHERENT IN CREATION

What, then, does this argument amount to? In short it comes to this. Every creature must be limited, and it is reasonable to suppose that a creature's perfection may be impossible, unless some frustration occurs in the earlier stages of its career. We can see that life could not go on in the world around us, unless living things preyed upon one another and, again, that man's social nature involves the possibility that the innocent may be harmed. The possibility of evil is inherent in creation, because the life of the highest creatures must be successive and progressive, and because what is not yet perfect may never become perfect. Yet, if evil is passing and good in the end prevails, and if the evil is less than the ultimate good, and inevitable if the good is to be gained, this eases very much the problem we are discussing.

The objection may be made that all I have done is to argue that the evil in the world may be inevitable if mankind is to be happy in the end, but that I have done very little to show why particular evils are inevitable. Indeed it may be said that many evils seem easily avoidable, without any apparent reason why any good should necessarily be forfeited as a result.

I should reply that we cannot expect to see in detail why evil is unavoidable if good is to follow. We cannot see the exact connection of cause and effect over the whole field of activity in the universe both visible and invisible: we have a very imperfect knowledge of the laws which govern either physical or spiritual events. My point is this. I have argued that it is not contradictory to say that God, though infinite in himself, cannot produce perfection of certain kinds in his creature unless some pain inevitably occurs in the process. We are not in a position to show how this applies to particular forms of evil; we can only say that they may be in fact inevitable, even though it appears that they could easily be avoided. At the same time the argument is of course strengthened if we can see, over limited sections of the field, why certain evils are inevitable if certain goods are to be secured. This I think we can do.

It may be worth adding a very general example of a possible connection between cause and effect. It is possible that the special kind of creation in which we live works out into its particular form as the result of one or two fundamental principles, from which all its other laws follow. It may be that, if a created thing is to be extended in space and time, our world with its special kind of beauty and happiness, but also with the possibility of special kinds of evil, must necessarily result. We can only conjecture, but the argument is supported if we can see *possible* reasons why evil is inevitable.

## ANIMAL PAIN

One other objection must be mentioned here, however briefly and inadequately. Your argument, it may be said, is that some evil may be necessary before a created thing can reach its final perfection, owing to this thing's particular nature. The end is realization of the highest powers in the highest degree possible. In this world the highest powers are those of man, and, if man is to be finally happy, you say that frustration in lower beings may be justified as a necessary means to this end. Now this theory may account for frustration in those lower beings which do not feel pain, but what of the pain of the higher animals? Is it not incompatible with God's loving providence that an animal should suffer and never reach its natural happiness, for the sake of man?

There is a special difficulty in dealing with this problem, because we have no certain knowledge of the kind of consciousness which animals possess. They appear to have a consciousness not entirely unlike our own but, since they cannot express themselves in words, the evidence is not clear. Undoubtedly there must be a great difference between our consciousness and theirs, and it is by no means easy to know what can be meant by a consciousness so very different from ours. We know what the consciousness of a child is, or that of a person who is half asleep, but what can be meant by consciousness less than human in a far more fundamental way? Moreover there is the further difficulty that living things below man shade down from the highest animals to the lowest organisms, with no clear line of division. But the lower we go the harder it is to see what consciousness can mean. Yet when are we to stop?

For these reasons animal pain does not seem to be a real problem in this connection, because we do not know exactly what has to be explained: there are no clear facts to produce a contradiction. Of course if animals have consciousness like human beings, they could not justly be treated as mere means for the good of man, but the evidence is against this. If they can feel pain at all like human beings, there is always the possibility that they may have some form of future life, when they will enjoy a happiness fully able to compensate for their pain. All we can say is that we do not know, but that the question does not concern us here, since it raises no difficulty against God's providence.

A few final remarks seem necessary before concluding this chapter. First, the reader may be surprised that I have not made more reference to the creature's power of free choice as an explanation of evil. Now there are two ways in which we can explain evil. We can do so either on the ground that it is inevitable in the working out of God's plan, or else on the ground that it results from the creature's free choice in opposition to God's plan. Each explanation has of course its own rather different set of problems. In this chapter I have been mainly discussing the first explanation, and shall go on to discuss the second. But I am not saying, it should be noticed, that any particular kind of evil, except when the implications are quite obvious, must be explained in one or the other of these ways; what I am arguing is that both are possible explanations of evil, and that both can be shown to be compatible with God's goodness and omnipotence. Probably we feel that one or other explanation seems more appropriate to certain kinds of evil. War, for example, or cruelty and oppression seem often better explained by free choice, while disease and natural calamities seem due to causes which are inevitable. Nevertheless there is plenty of room for doubt. Some natural evils may be ultimately due to the sins of men, or of angels who have charge of the visible creation. On the other hand the scope of free choice may be much narrower than at first sight appears. I am not attempting to decide such questions here; I am arguing that both explanations are possible.

It may be useful to put the problem in the form of the question, so often asked: Why does not God, if he is all-good and almighty, put us in a better world, where there are fewer evils than in this? The answer I am suggesting is that this would be impossible, because the idea of his doing so is meaningless. God wills to create each individual human being, that each may reach his perfection and be happy. Now every human being is (apart from the effects of his free choice) the product of his environment and of the history of the world. No individual could exist in an entirely different environment, in a different world, because he would not be the same individual. The world, however, in which we find ourselves, and without which we could not exist, itself could not exist without the kind of evils we are considering. They are inevitable, if the world is to reach its special perfection. In the end we can be sure that good will prevail for all who do not deliberately choose evil, because God would not have a purpose which could not be fulfilled. God guides all things in the world towards the final happiness of all who have not rejected this, permitting the evil which is unavoidable in the process of development, for the sake of the end in view.

At the risk of repetition I should like to make it clear again in conclusion that the explanation of evil just given is only one explanation. The other explanation which seems to me possible, and which I next turn to, is that it is due to free choice. Perhaps both are possible explanations, and some evil may be explained in the one way and some in the other. But if the reader thinks that probably all evil is due to free choice, then the first explanation ceases to be necessary. It only remains necessary as an explanation of the possibility of free choice itself: we shall have to say that God permits the possibility of free choice, with the danger of sin which it involves, because this is unavoidable if there is to be the possibility of supreme good.

# CHAPTER V

# SIN

We come to the more difficult part of the problem, and must consider evil, not when it is inevitable in the working out of God's plan, but when it is the result of the creature's free choice and is in opposition to God's plan.

Before outlining the theory which I shall defend, I mention briefly the two theories which have been most widely held by Catholic theologians. I shall only mention them briefly because it seems clear that at the present time neither theory is held with great conviction, and indeed the tendency is to leave the problem alone as insoluble. For example Tanquerey, in his *Synopsis Theologiae Dogmaticae*, gives as an example of a mystery of the natural order the harmonizing of human freedom with God's foreknowledge, and even Fr Joyce, in his generally admirable book, *Principles of Natural Theology*, discussing the question of God's concurrence with the action of the free creature, concludes (p. 553): "But how is it that man determines himself to abstain from corresponding with one premotion and to admit another? Here is the mystery of free will, and of this we have no explanation to offer. We can described the conditions of the faculty's exercise, but cannot explain the act itself." Fr Garrigou-Lagrange in his book *De Deo Uno*, although he does not commit himself explicitly, travels far along this path. When he has reached the crucial point and has formulated his answer, he adds (p. 545): "This indeed is a most obscure assertion", *haec propositio quidem est obscurissima.*

Nevertheless such an attitude to the problem seems to have the most serious consequences. We have to remember that it is not merely a question of investigating a set of events, and seeing how much we can discover about their causes and how much is hidden. It is a question of showing that two assertions which we make involve no contradiction. We affirm that God exists and is almighty, and also that creatures exist and do evil. If we offer no reconciliation a very serious gap remains in our argument for the existence of God.

There have, as is well known, been two main answers given to this question by Catholic theologians, one by the Molinists and one by the Thomists. The objection to Molinism is that it appears to give a positive priority to the creature in the act of free choice, and thus to attribute to the creature an activity not traceable to God as its source. God seems to be determined by the act of the creature, which would undermine the whole argument for God's existence. The objection to the Thomist solution is that, while it is careful to make God the source of all activity, it does not appear to leave room for human free choice.

## THE MOLINIST SOLUTION

Luis de Molina (1535–1600), a Jesuit at the time of the Reformation, set himself to defend the power of the will to choose freely, and at the same time to harmonize this with the efficacy of divine grace. After much controversy with the Thomists the dispute settled down to the question how God could have knowledge of future free acts so as to give grace only when he knows a man will cooperate. For the Molinists held that efficacious grace included the free consent of the will, and had to explain how God's decree to bestow efficacious grace must necessarily attain its end. They argued, therefore, that God knows what choice each human will would make in any given circumstances, and hence can bestow grace with infallible certainty of its effective use. But how can God have such knowledge? The distinction had already been made between God's knowledge of merely possible things and his knowledge of things which at some time would actually be realized, the former being called *scientia simplicis intelligentiae*, knowledge of pure understanding, the latter being called *scientia visionis*, knowledge of sight. To explain how God could know what choice would be made by the human will in every different set of circumstances the term *scientia media*, mediate knowledge, was invented, on the ground that the way in which the human will would act was more than a merely possible event and less than a real event.

The obvious objection to this theory was that it made it very difficult to explain how the human will remained free, if God foreknew what it would do in every conceivable set of circumstances. Suarez, therefore, another Jesuit, rejected this explanation of God's mediate knowledge, and maintained that God had this knowledge by knowing both the decree by which he concurs with the realization of free acts, and also the part which the free will is to play in realizing them. But does this solve the problem? Many theologians have thought it does not, among them Fr Joyce, who thinks it impossible to explain why on some occasions a man does not correspond with God's action upon him, while on other occasions he does, if human volition depends absolutely on the divine "premotion" or causality.

## THE THOMIST SOLUTION

On the other hand the Thomist theologians started, so to speak, from the other end: they clung firmly to the belief that God was always the master, and that no causality could be exercised apart from him, and their difficulties arose when they came to explain human free choice. For them there was not the same difficulty about God's foreknowledge of freely chosen future events, because they held that God knew everything in the decrees by which he determined what should happen. But the question was, if God determines the human act, how is man responsible? The suggestion was made that God determines the act, but also gives man his free manner of acting. The objection, however, to this is that a manner of acting which allows for free choice is precisely a manner of acting which excludes determination from any other agent than the human will itself—in other words, that the suggestion is contradictory.

It is interesting to see the form the problem takes in the hands of Fr Garrigou-Lagrange, a defender of the strict Thomist view. In the end he reduces the issue to the question of man's condemnation to eternal punishment. He tells us that God permits man's reprobation on account of man's free choice of sin, but he says that this permission is given *ante praevisa demerita* (*De Deo Uno*, p. 543); that is, in logical order the permission is first given and the sin follows after. His ground for saying this is of course that otherwise God's absolute sovereignty is infringed, and his free gift of grace and salvation denied. Fr Garrigou-Lagrange is clear that the sin is not the motive for God's permission of reprobation: "Since negative reprobation is nothing else than the will to permit that some shall fail to attain glory, and since permission for the sin of the wicked precedes this sin, this sin cannot be its motive." Why, then, does God permit sin? "On account of the greater good involved in the manifestation of the splendour of infinite justice." It is this assertion which he admits to be *propositio obscurissima*, though he claims that to deny it is impossible (p. 545). He further explains: "God does not will to permit the sin through love for, and intention of, finite punishment, for this would be against justice. But, through the intention of manifesting infinite justice, or the inviolable right of the Supreme Good to be loved above all things, first he wills to permit the sin, and then he wills to inflict the punishment of the sin for the manifestation of justice" (p. 548).

The weak points in this theory are plain: it is putting the cart before the horse. God is said to permit sin and decree punishment in order to manifest his justice, but it seems to be forgotten that the very notion of justice in this connection implies that permission of sin and decree of punishment should result from the wrongful will of the sinner. Justice in regard to sin is giving the sinner what he deserves; it can never be the end for which sin may be permitted. Sin of its nature is opposed to God; it would always be better if the sin did not take place, and no punishment was required. If we say that God permits sin in order to manifest his justice, this surely implies that God wills sin for some further purpose, which is contradictory. Moreover God can manifest his justice by rewarding virtue as well as by punishing vice. I shall return later to this question of God's justice and of punishment.

## A PROPOSAL

Therefore strict Molinism and extreme Thomism both seem to suffer from insurmountable difficulties. I shall now go on to propose a solution which is rather different, but yet is, I think, in harmony with the main principles of scholasticism. Other solutions have so much against them, and this (I shall argue) so much in its favour in spite of difficulties which are inevitable in such a subject, that it is surprising that it should be usually neglected. At least it should be fully discussed before being rejected. This is an attempt to prevent the case going by default.

To introduce the theory I must refer to what was said in the last chapter. We have to speak of God as possessing knowledge, but we have to explain that in fact his knowledge is identical with the simple, eternal, act of his being. We can speak of God's knowledge but this, though true, is inadequate. However, allowing for this, we can say that God knows from eternity, and that there is no question of God having fore-knowledge in any temporal sense, since his knowledge of events is always simultaneous with the events themselves. It comes to this: if we can explain in terms of causality how God is the first cause and yet creatures have free choice, no further problem arises as to God's knowledge, for his knowledge is simply awareness of what exists.

It may be best to sum up at once the solution I am proposing, so that the reader can see its general outline from the beginning. It may be put very briefly as follows. When the creature sins, this is ultimately due, not to any positive act initiated by the creature without God's causality, but to a failure on the creature's part to do all that he has the power to do. So far as the creature fails and acts less perfectly than he could act, this is due to a mere lack of causality, and is the responsibility of the creature and not of God. That is the essence of the theory I shall try to argue. Of course what I have just said is admitted by all theologians, but they do not go on to find in this principle the solution to the problem as a whole. What I have to show is that it does provide a key to the whole problem. I shall argue that God permits the creature's failure, if it occurs, because such permission is unavoidable if there is to be the possibility of supreme happiness. He permits his own causal act to be restricted in view of the creature's failure: the creature's failure has a negative priority over the intensity of God's causal act upon the creature.

# CHAPTER VI

# THE PROPOSED SOLUTION

Let us begin by asking why a man, if he chooses, chooses one course rather than another, or, in other words, what is meant by choice. The difficulty is familiar. If a choice is possible, this must be because there is a conflict of desires. But, if the desires are equally strong, what makes us choose one rather than another, while, if one is stronger, how can there be any possibility of choice at all? If it is replied that we ourselves make our desire stronger when we choose, then the question is, why do we make it stronger? Must not this be due to some further desire which determines us? In other words, must not every action have a cause or motive, and, if this is so, what room is left for choice?

## CHOICE LIES BETWEEN A GREATER AND A LESSER GOOD

Now I suggest that, whenever a choice is possible, the choice lies between a greater good, some end which will perfect us and realize our powers more fully, and a lesser good, some end which will perfect us and realize our powers less fully. For example, we may have conflicting desires for physical and intellectual satisfaction, for satisfaction at the present moment and over a longer period of time, for personal satisfaction and the satisfaction of others. Desires may shade down from desire for ultimate satisfaction of the highest kind for all creatures, that is, desire that God's will shall be fully carried out, to desire for personal satisfaction of the lowest kind at the present moment. Thus desires may be related to one another as greater to less, since they may seek a wider and more permanent, or a narrower and more passing satisfaction. When choice is possible, I am suggesting that it always lies between a greater and a lesser desire.

Of course choice may be possible, not between desire for the highest good and desire for the lowest good, but also between desires for different degrees of value between these extremes. Nor does choice necessarily lie between the more immediate and the less immediate attractions; two attractions may both be immediate, but one of greater value than the other —for example, because the good of more people is involved.

But do we not often choose between good of quite equal value? It seems to me that many of the apparently free choices of everyday life are not really choices at all, because they are only the selection of means to an end already determined. If, for example, we are planning a holiday, the arrangements are not so much a matter of choice, as of finding out what we shall enjoy. A genuine choice can only be made when there are conflicting desires for different ends. If we are only deciding the best means to reach an end already settled, there can be no real choice, because the decision depends simply on our ability to discover the best means to reach the end. But how can choice be explained when objects of equal value are desired? I suggest that no choice between them is possible; to decide between them we must take one or the other at random, choosing to do this because it is a greater good to take one at random than to do nothing at all.

But how (it may be said)—even granting this is true—does it help to explain choice? All we have been asked to accept so far is that choice always lies between a greater and a lesser good. But what makes a man choose one or the other? Why is not the desire for the greater good always the stronger?

From different points of view either the greater or the lesser good may appear more attractive, and a real conflict of desires may arise. The greater good has greater value in the end, but it may be more remote, and may involve trouble or suffering at the present time. The lesser good has less value in the end, but it may give more immediate pleasure at the moment. In so far as a man expands his field of vision to its fullest extent, he desires the highest good; in so far as he lets his vision contract and his attention focus on his personal and immediate interest alone, he desires the lowest good.

But why does he either expand or contract his attention; what is it which makes him choose one or the other? If he chooses the greater good, then the answer is straightforward. He expands his attention to the fullest extent because he has the power to do so, and because causes have acted upon him, and have enabled him to realize this power. The motives and reasons which have prompted him are sufficient to account for his course of action. But, if he chooses the lower good instead of the higher, there is no need to look for a cause beyond the man himself, since a failure as such is negative, and what is negative, as such, requires no cause. Of course there is a positive cause and a sufficient motive for his taking the lesser good, in so far as it has positive value, but there is no cause, only a lack of cause, for his taking the lesser good instead of the greater good, for his failure to take the greater good.

There must always be a positive reason for a positive act, nor have we given the reason fully until we have traced it back to God. But, if we ask why a failure takes place, in the nature of the case no positive answer can be given. Therefore I am suggesting that we need look for no cause beyond the man himself who fails, to account for his choice of the lesser good.

But must not less causation have been given to the man, if his action is less than it might have been? Is not the cause of his failure the lack of activity in the causes acting upon him, and consequently are not these causes responsible for the failure, and not the man himself? It is undoubtedly true that, if a purely material thing fails, its failure is due to a corresponding lack of activity in the causes which produce it; we can trace the failure to something beyond the thing itself. Here, however, we are not speaking of purely material things, but of human beings. A human being is conscious of himself and of other objects, of his own powers, and of the purpose and results of his action, thereby controlling his conduct in a way quite different from that of a merely material thing. Every independent thing is in a sense a source of activity, but man is so in a very special sense. Therefore it seems reasonable to claim that, although the failure of a piece of metal can always be traced to failure in causes outside itself, nevertheless failure in a human being originates in the human being himself. We are dealing with human beings, and all must at least agree that they control their actions in a special way. We are trying to explain choice, and all must at least agree that there are strong arguments for the reality of choice. Admittedly explanation is difficult, but in favour of the present theory it may be claimed that a meaning is given to choice, and contradiction is avoided. If a man chooses the better course, all causality is accounted for without raising any problem. If he chooses the worse course, his failure as such is explained as due to a lack of action on his part, which need not be traced beyond himself; it requires no reason or motive to account for it, but only a lack of reason or motive.

## CHOICE BETWEEN GOOD AND EVIL

There is an important point to be added. So far I have been speaking of choice between a greater and a lesser good, and I must now apply what has been said to choice between good and evil. If the choice lies between good and evil, this means that it lies between a greater good and a lesser good, but a lesser good which leads to frustration. Choice may lie between a greater good and a lesser good which is merely less perfect than the greater good, without involving any frustration, while it may also lie between good and evil. Of course the choice can never lie between good and pure evil, because evil cannot exist by itself. Choice must always lie between a greater good and a lesser good, but this lesser good may be such as to lead to frustration. We can only act if we have a desire to act, and we can only have a desire for a positive end, though that positive end may be such as to involve ultimately frustration. Hence, when evil is chosen, there is a positive motive and reason for the choice, but the positive good does not cause ultimate good.

Now, if this theory about free choice is sound, we must go on to ask if it helps us to reconcile the creature's choice of evil with God's absolute causality. The contradiction arises plainly if the choice of evil means that the creature initiates positive action, uncaused by God. If, however, it only means that the creature initiates failure, while all that is positive is caused by God, the problem is less difficult. In that case all that has to be explained is how a creature can, through his own fault, fail to act up to his full powers.

The answer I propose follows from what has been said. A failure to act, being as such merely negative, requires no cause, and can therefore originate in the creature who fails, without our needing to trace it further. When the creature chooses an evil course he chooses a positive good, but one which will lead to frustration. In so far as he chooses a positive good his action is caused by God; in so far as he chooses a lesser good than is possible, and one that leads to frustration, his action is due to himself alone. Hence God is always the cause of good, but the creature alone is responsible for evil.

Many objections will at once spring to the reader's mind, but perhaps the following goes to the heart of the matter. Does not this theory leave us in the old difficulty? For either God causes the creature's sin by giving less perfection than he might have given, thereby causing the creature to fail, or else the creature determines God's causality in a positive way. When the creature fails he performs another act instead of the act that he might have performed. If the creature's failure is due only to the creature himself, does not this imply that God is forced to 'premove', that is, determine, the creature to another positive act, to which he would not otherwise have premoved him?

This objection is answered if I can show that there is no such implication, that the creature by his failure does not determine God's causality positively, but only negatively. If I can show this both horns of the dilemma will be avoided. On the one hand, it will be clear that God does not cause the creature to fail by giving less less perfection than was possible, but that God gives less perfection on account of the creature's failure. On the other hand, it will be clear that, though the creature is the ultimate source of the failure, yet he is only a negative source.

It is essential to remember that in God's premotion of a creature there is no question of *temporal* precedence of God's causal act over the effect produced in the creature; it is only a question of *logical* precedence. Thus God sees the failure in the creature and premoves it accordingly, but simultaneously with the failure; God upholds the creature in being, but he upholds a creature which has in it a failure, a flaw, a negation. God limits his causality in view of this failure, just as he limits his causality in view of the creature's natural limits. But how does the failure arise, if the creature is wholly in God's power? All that is positive in the creature is derived from God, but what God upholds is precisely a free creature, a creature which has the power to originate from itself a failure, or, to speak more accurately, the power simply not to act. God allows his own premotion to be determined negatively by the creature. Even this phrase "determined negatively" is inaccurate. A determination is something positive, but all that the creature contributes from itself is negative. It is more accurate to say simply that God premoves to a lesser act on account of the creature's failure. To determine an act is to do something positive, and in so far as an act is less when it might be greater this is due to nothing positive, but to a mere lack of determination. What we ought to say is that there is *less premotion* on account of the creature's failure.

An opponent may object that the difficulty has not been met. If the creature performs act B, which is less than act A, when it might have performed act A, there must be a positive premotion to act B instead of to act A. God therefore, it may be said, is positively determined by the creature to premove it to act B instead of to act A, and this is contradictory, since God cannot be positively determined by a creature. The answer is that the term of God's causal act is less as a result of the creature's failure, but that this does not imply that God is determined. As a result of the lesser degree of determination which God gives to the creature God premoves to act B, but the fact that it is act B is due to the particular order in the world as created by God. What I mean is this. There are laws of physical cause and effect which, apart from free choice, determine the whole succession of events. Suppose a man has to choose between sitting in his chair or getting up and doing some work he ought to do. If the man does what he is capable of doing, he gets up and works. If he does less than he is capable of doing, he stays still. His choice results in one of two quite different acts. If God gives a greater degree of premotion to the man, he works (act A); if less, he sits still (act B). If God premoves to act B, God is not determined by the creature positively to premove to act B. God produces a lesser effect in the man on account of his failure, and, since the effect is less and God has created a certain order in the world, God therefore premoves to act B. The fact that it is act B is entirely due to God's order in the world; all that the creature has originated of himself is a mere negation, a mere failure.

We have to remember, too, that, when God premoves a creature, this does not mean that a new act occurs in God corresponding to the effect in the creature. When *we* act and produce an external effect, we do so by producing a new act in ourselves proportionate to the effect. This is not so with God since he is infinite in power, and since there can be but one simple unchanging act in God. We can only think of God as though he were a creature, and then remember that our thought must be raised to infinity where all perfection, all different acts, are in reality one simple act. Hence, when we think of God's causal act on creatures, we have to remember that in reality there is no new act in God corresponding to a particular effect in the creature. Consequently when, owing to the creature's failure, God gives less premotion, this does not mean that there is any diminution of act in God, it only means that there is a diminution—or rather, some unrealized power —in the creature. And thus we see again that failure may be due entirely to the creature, and yet that God may not be determined by the creature.

The point at which the theory here proposed conflicts with the Thomist view as put forward by Fr Garrigou-Lagrange is seen clearly when we come to the motive for God's decree of damnation. The rigorous Thomist school holds, as I have said, that God permits the punishment of the creature *ante praevisa demerita*, that is, in logical order before the occurrence of the sin. The view here proposed is that God permits the punishment *post praevisa demerita*, that is, in logical order after the occurrence of the sin. Undoubtedly it is true that God gives all grace and perfection in logical order before any virtuous act occurs, because all that is positive must be caused by God. But it does not follow that this is true of punishment. If the theory I have suggested is correct the creature's failure has a negative priority (not of course of time, but of logical order) over God's causal act.

## ANSWERS TO CERTAIN OBJECTIONS

The following points may be worth adding in support of the argument.

First, God sees the whole life of the creature simultaneously in his own eternity, yet he sees it as it really is, as events in time, one act following another. We have some notion of how this can be from our knowledge of past events which happened successively, and which we know all together. If we bear this in mind, it makes it easier to understand how God can permit the creature to fail through his own fault. God gives him a nature which involves this power, and therefore allows his own act of causality, as it proceeds in the creature, to become less than it might have been on account of the creature's failure. From the point of view of eternity, however, God simply gives an act of causality which is limited by the creature's nature and freely chosen limitations. Nor is there any question of God waiting to see how the creature will choose; God sees the whole of what happens simultaneously with its occurrence. Nor is God passive in any sense to the creature's action, since all that the creature of itself is responsible for is a negation, a failure, nothing positive. God gives a premotion which he permits to be defective on account of the failure in the creature which he simultaneously perceives. He premoves the creature from eternity to the lesser act.

Secondly, all theologians agree that God "permits" sin, since if we said he willed it we should be involved in contradiction: sin is what opposes God's will. St Thomas tells us: "It is also a part of divine providence that [God] should permit some to fail to reach their end, and this is to reject them" (*Summa Theol.* Ia, Qu. 23, art. 3, *c*). Now what is involved in saying that God "permits" sin? God permits free choice to occur, because it is inevitable, if the good is to be achieved, and therefore is part of his plan, in spite of the fact that a wrong choice may be made, and sin may be committed. But sin itself is not a necessary evil which God permits as inevitable, as part of his plan, in order that good shall be achieved. If, then, God permits sin, this must mean that he permits a cause to operate which he does not cause himself, since it opposes his plan. To permit sin means to refrain from stopping it, and hence it implies that there is a cause operating which is not caused by God. But there cannot be any positive cause which is not caused by God, and so it must be a negative cause, a failure, as I have argued. It seems, therefore, that implicitly all theologians admit a negative priority in the creature's failure over God's premotion. After all we cannot get away from the fact that sin opposes God's will, and can only be permitted, and in no sense positively willed, by God.

Thirdly, a few words should be said on this objection: Is not every sinful act a positive act, even though it may lead to frustration? But is not a positive act caused by God? How can God be said to will an act of cruelty? I should reply that we cannot simply say, without making any distinction either that God wills and causes an act of cruelty, or that he does not. The act of cruelty is the product of God's causality and of the creature's failure, and these are independent factors, which together produce the act of cruelty. God's causality is deflected so to speak, by the failure initiated by the creature.

Fourthly, how can we separate negative from positive priority? If the creature is responsible for his own failures, must he not also be responsible for his success? If on a given occasion he succeeds when he has the power to fail, must not this be due to his own efforts alone? I cannot, however, see that this follows. If the creature continues to do right, though having the power to fail, this is due to the positive strength he possesses, which is derived from God. The fact that he does not fail is only incidental to the fact that he does right. It is only his weakness, if he fails, that he alone brings about. I may put it like this: the normal situation is that the creature shall act rightly, and then this is caused wholly by God. This normal situation can be affected negatively by failure initiated by the creature. It is only in so far as the normal situation is affected in this way that the creature is ultimately responsible. Thus what determines the creature to do a right action is the causality of God together with the absence of failure on the part of the creature. What determines the creature to do a wrong action is the causality of God together with failure on the part of the creature. In either case the creature initiates nothing positive.

For the sake of clearness it may be useful to sum up the argument of this chapter to the present point. Choice is possible for the creature, because his desire for the greater good may conflict with his desire for the lesser good, because what is ultimately the greater good may involve immediate difficulties not involved in what is ultimately the lesser good. Choice arises because the greater good is not greater from every point of view, although the creature is aware that it is really the greater. If he lets his attention slip from the greater to the lesser good, and acts accordingly, there is no reason for his failure beyond himself. Of course choice implies that the mind can be aware of two different attractions at the same time, and that the attention can focus on one of the attractions, while still aware of the other at the edge, so to speak, of the consciousness. If the creature fails, this happens because God allows him to have a negative priority over God's act of causality; God modifies his causality in accordance with the creature's failure. This does not mean that the creature is outside God's control in any sense which contradicts God's supreme authority, since God sees the failure from eternity, and plans subsequent events in creation in view of the failure which for good reasons he permits.

This is the theory I am suggesting, and, to complete it, the question must now be considered, Why does God give the creature the power of free choice? Why does he allow the creature to have this power to sin, and thereby bring in so many evils? Why does he not make sure that every creature will always do what is right?

## WHY DOES GOD GIVE THE CREATURE THE POWER OF FREE CHOICE?

Plainly we shall have to reply that God allows free choice with its attendant dangers because this is inevitable if his plan for the ultimate good and happiness of creatures is to be realized. There can surely be no other explanation than this. But we are still left with the problem, Why is free choice inevitable if this end is to be achieved? Now to this we are entitled to reply that there must be a reason, although we do not know, or, at least, cannot be sure, what it is. For our knowledge of the laws which govern the working out of human destiny is very restricted. Nevertheless I think we can in fact go further than this, and see plausible reasons which may explain why the possibility of failure is necessary.

God creates man that in the end he may enjoy supreme happiness through the beatific vision, for God has given him the supernatural power which is necessary for this supreme perfection. Thus man has been given an intellect, with consciousness of the purpose of his own actions, and control, in dependence on God, of his own conduct. This is the basis on which man's higher spiritual powers rest. Nothing but the infinite can fully satisfy man's aspirations. No finite object can satisfy his desires and thus compel him to act, because he is aware of a greater good.

Now the possibility of man's failure in the present life seems to follow as a consequence of this. I have suggested already that a creature, capable of supreme perfection, must be perfected by a process, however short, involving the succession of one event after another, before the beatific vision is attained. That is man's state in the present life. He is aware obscurely, though with sufficient clearness, of the attraction of the infinite good, and hence that he ought to frame his conduct in accordance with God's plan which will lead him to unity with God. At the same time he is aware of the attraction of finite goods, the enjoyment of which may sometimes be contrary to God's plan. He is aware of himself as having a real but finite value, and of God as having supreme value. But he is not yet fully united to God, and the present good may conflict with the ultimate good. A conflict of desires is possible simply because the end is not yet reached. Hence at this stage of his career man may be faced with situations in which neither right conduct, which will lead to final satisfaction, satisfies all his desires at the present moment, nor does wrong conduct do so. It is this condition of affairs which makes choice possible, and this condition of affairs may in some measure be inevitable during the process of perfection before the end is attained. It does not follow necessarily that choice is always inevitable for every creature, but only that, when a creature does have to make the choice between right and wrong conduct, this is permitted by God because in the circumstances it is inevitable. It is possible that in certain different circumstances some creatures may be able to avoid the need for exposure to such strong desires for wrong conduct that a choice has to be made.

I suggest, therefore, that we can see in outline possible reasons why God permits the danger of failure, when he does so. It is because the best interests of the creature then make it unavoidable.

In its ultimate form the question may be put in this way: How can there be even the possibility of evil, if God is utterly good? How can even the very idea have ever appeared? In view of what has just been said the answer I should make is plain. There can be no possibility of evil in God himself, and the idea is unthinkable in connection with him. But the possibility of evil is necessarily involved in creation. Just because God is infinite and all-good any separation from him involves the possibility of evil, and creation, because it is creation and involves a process of perfection before full union with God is realized, implies a certain separation while the process is still unfinished. Thus it seems reasonable to think that the possibility of evil is inseparable from creation.

In point of fact I should be inclined to go further. It seems arguable that some degree of pain is not only necessarily possible, but necessarily actual, if there are to be creatures capable of the highest perfection. Sin, that is to say, evil due to free choice, is necessarily possible, but never of course necessarily actual; with pain it is different. For, if choice is inevitable, there must be a conflict of desires preceding the act of choice, and a conflict of desires is of its very nature in some degree painful; one desire must be suppressed when the will makes its choice.

# CHAPTER VII

# SOME FURTHER

# QUESTIONS

I begin this chapter by discussing an objection of a rather different type against the theory I have been defending. This theory argues that the creature has been given free choice, not because it is valuable in itself, but because it is unavoidable if there is to be the possibility of supreme perfection. Thus the power to choose between right and wrong conduct is regarded rather as a necessary evil than a good, since it involves the danger of failure.

Now the objection may be raised that this theory misses the true value of free choice. Is not the power to choose freely an essential element in personality? Is it not precisely virtue freely chosen which gives value to conduct, and does not this imply that the creature must be able to initiate positively its choice of good? This would mean that the suggestion that the creature is only responsible for failure misses the whole point, because it does not recognize the real value of free choice.

Against such an objection I should begin by arguing that it would be contradictory to hold that the creature could initiate a positive act. If the creature could do this he would be the ultimate cause in some true sense of his action, and God alone can be the ultimate cause of activity. It would mean that the creature was not a creature, dependent on God, but was nothing else than God, the first cause. Nor can God give such a power to a creature, because it would be equivalent to making a second God, which is meaningless. There seems no way of meeting this argument, provided we agree that God exists, infinite in perfection, and therefore the source of all reality.

Therefore, if we accept the existence of God, we must agree that the creature, that is to say, every finite being, is wholly dependent on God, and consequently that every virtue which the creature possesses is received from God. That is why we seem forced to conclude that the creature is only responsible for failure and not, in ultimate analysis, for the virtues derived from God. For this reason I should maintain that it cannot be free choice which gives value to conduct, because every thing that is valuable must be caused by God, and cannot be ultimately due to the creature.

Nevertheless there seems to be an important truth contained in the objection, and we must try to see what it is and how it can be accounted for by the theory I have proposed. Perhaps the reason why the valuable element in conduct is thought to be virtue self-originated, is that conduct is assumed to be the full expression of personality only if it is the result of self-originated choice. But is this so? Undoubtedly conduct cannot have its full value as the expression of the individual personality unless there is full knowledge and deliberation, together with a clear realization of the purpose in view—unless, in short, it is fully the act of the person himself and not the product of his environment. Yet surely these conditions can be fulfilled when no choice has to be made. Choice arises from a conflict of desires, but an act can be the full expression of individual personality when all desires point in one direction. It is difficult to see why it should be better for a man to have desires for wrong conduct as well as right conduct than to have desires for right conduct alone. We have to remember that in the beatific vision, when the creature is fully united with God and sees God face to face, there can be no possibility of wrong desires, and yet personality is realized then to the full.

In order that personality may be realized what is required is that the right desires should be present, and that these should be followed with full understanding and full committal on the part of the will. This means that what is required is virtue. Now the essential virtue is the love of the good, the love of God, because this leads to all other virtues. Therefore love of God is the really important element in conduct, through which personality is expressed, and not choice, however we explain choice. Personality is expressed through union with God which comes about by love of God.

The reply may be made that it is plainly true that love of God is essential to good human conduct, but that this virtue is only practised in the present life, or at least only practised to its fullest extent, when there are difficulties to be surmounted, and when in spite of them the right course has to be chosen—that it is in the choice of good when we are tempted towards evil that the love of God is in fact shown. If this is what is meant no doubt there is much truth in it. No one can deny that, under the conditions of life in this world, virtue is normally developed through contact with difficulties, and that the will for good usually becomes more deliberate, a fuller expression of the personality, the more it involves a struggle. But the question we have to ask is whether it is only under the conditions of this life that the love of God is usually best developed after a difficult choice, or whether this is necessarily and always the case. It is hard to see why there should be a necessary connection between choice and a fully personal act of the love of God. We are brought back to the question: Can we fully commit ourselves to seeking to realize a desire, when we have no contrary desire? It is true that often in this life a struggle with contrary desires focuses the mind and will and makes an act more deliberate. But there seems no reason why desire for a given end should not be stimulated simply by intense awareness of its attractiveness. When this is so, and when there are no contrary desires and when there is no question of choice, conduct can surely be deliberate and fully express individual personality.

These remarks provide the opportunity to reply to certain objections against free choice which I mentioned in the first chapter. In view of what has just been said I can now give my answer. The difficulties are those raised by Rashdall, who claims that indeterminism leads to absurdities. It would mean, he says, that no virtues due to heredity or upbringing or good example were of real value, and consequently that there could be no moral value in helping others or teaching them or giving them good example, since only what they do of their independent choice could really matter.

Now this argument undoubtedly seems to show that choice is not the valuable element in character, in the sense that only by acts of choice do we fully commit ourselves and express our personality. If this were so, Rashdall's arguments would apply, and we should be driven to the conclusion that good influence on others was useless, because only what comes from ourselves alone would be valuable. On the other hand this argument does not show that we do not possess the power of choice, if choice does not lead to the absurdities to which Rashdall thinks that it leads. We have good reasons, as I have already said, for believing that we have free choice, the good reasons being our direct experience and the conclusions contrary to common sense which a denial involves. We have strong grounds for accepting it, but we must try to meet the arguments on the other side.

The question, then, is: Does belief in free choice lead to absurdities, as Rashdall thinks? The theory that I have been defending maintains that all that is positively good in character is derived from God, while only failure is due to man himself. It follows that, although choice is really possible, it is not an essential element in fully human conduct. An act may be virtuous, it may be an act of the love of God, and it may express the individual personality, while being the result of God's causality and not due to any ultimate causality on man's part. Whether it results from choice or not makes no difference. For, even if it results from choice, all the good that is chosen is caused by God, and only in a dependent sense by the man who chooses. Consequently choice is not essential to the highest kind of conduct, but may rather be described as an incidental but unfortunate necessity when it occurs. What is essential to the highest kind of conduct is that it should be fully conscious and deliberate, and should have as its motive the love of God.

Hence we can answer Rashdall's argument as follows. All that a man receives from others by good example, teaching, and so on, far from being useless, is truly valuable to him if it increases his love of God, for this and not personal choice is the essential element in good conduct. It is always produced by God's causality and is, therefore, no less valuable when it comes through the example or teaching of another man than when it does not do so. On the other hand the man who lacks the good he might have had if a good influence had affected him is really not so good as he would have been had he had the benefit of such an influence and had profited from it, for he has less love of God, even though through no fault of his own.

It may be felt: Surely this is unjust? Does it not mean that a man's degree of goodness does not depend on himself? How, then, can he be judged? I should reply as follows. This is no more mysterious or unjust than the general fact that different men have different talents and opportunities. A man is only judged in accordance with the opportunities he has had, and is only blamed for failure, when he fails through his own fault. If a man does the best he can in spite of a bad natural disposition, justice of course requires that in the end he should be perfected and should be happy in whatever degree of perfection is possible to him. Justice does not require that everyone should have an equal capacity for perfection, or even that everyone should have equal opportunities for reaching his particular degree. It only requires that in the end each person shall have what is due to him. What I am arguing is that the love of God is a fully personal act and is the valuable element in conduct, but that it is produced through God's causality. A man is good in the spiritual sense in so far as he possesses the love of God, which God has given him; he is bad in so far as he lacks the love of God through his own fault, and he can lack it through his own fault because failure is negative.

Thus I may put my answer to Rashdall in this way.

First, I am not defending an indeterminism, in which man positively determines himself, with no further cause beyond himself. I am defending an explanation of free choice which gives man only the power to initiate failure.

Secondly, to say what a man would choose freely to do, when in fact he has never made the choice, is meaningless.

Thirdly, the valuable element in conduct is love of God, willed by a fully personal act. It makes no essential difference whether such an act is the result of free choice or not, because in any case it is caused by God. It is no less valuable because it is caused by God and not initiated ultimately by the creature.

Fourthly, the wrong element in conduct is the creature's failure to do all that he was capable of doing.

It seems worth pointing out that these objections of Rashdall against indeterminism are an indirect argument in favour of the view of free choice I am defending. For the objections make a strong case against an indeterminism which says that man can initiate positive action, and that therefore his self-determination is the valuable element in his conduct. Yet at the same time there is also a strong case in favour of some kind of free choice. The theory which explains free choice as due simply to the power to fail, if it can be established, steers a passage between these opposing difficulties.

I will now develop what I have just been saying by showing how it applies in various ways.

It enables us to understand how God can strengthen a man's will for good by his grace, without in any way lowering the value of the resulting conduct. God can directly premove a man to follow his good desires more strongly and can intensify the good desires. There is no contradiction—at least from the standpoint we are considering—in the idea of a man's being freed even in the present life from all evil desires and premoved to good action, and so being prevented from choice, while still enjoying the full use of his will and of all the highest and most valuable elements in human conduct.

God, then, can strengthen the will; it remains to ask whether he can so strengthen a man as to make him *choose* rightly. There can be little hesitation in replying that this is contradictory. To make a man choose rightly is to take away his power of choice, since to choose is to do something without being made to do it. Choice, however, can certainly be influenced from outside. For choice is only possible when there is a conflict of desires, and choice of a line of conduct is easier if desire for it is stronger. Therefore, although it is contradictory to speak of God's determining the will directly in the exercise of choice, there is a perfectly true sense in which he can strengthen the will indirectly in its choice by increasing the desire for good and so making a good choice easier.

If all this is true it serves to throw light on the reason why we pray not to be led into temptation. At first we are inclined to feel, as I have said, that the really valuable element in human conduct lies in the choice of good when there exists a tendency to evil, and that virtue must be the outcome of struggle, since if there is no tendency to evil we are forced mechanically towards the good. I have argued that man is no more independent when he chooses good after a struggle than when he does so with no tendency to evil at all, for in both cases his action depends on God. The fact that in the former case he might have failed makes no difference whatever. Then why, it might be asked, are we so inclined to feel that the highest virtue is only shown in trial and temptation?

First, no doubt because we imagine a man is more independent when he makes a choice. I have already argued against this. Secondly, we are apt to confuse temptation and pain. Pain may be an occasion for the practice of virtue, but may occur without any temptation to evil. Thirdly, in the circumstances of our present life the stimulus of struggle is sometimes accidentally—though not necessarily—the means through which virtue is developed; in other words, temptation is almost equivalent to training. Fourthly, we may confuse the situation in which man has the opportunity to do wrong yet chooses to do the good, all the time being firm in virtue and free from any strong desire for evil, and the situation in which he has a strong desire for evil. In the first case the man is only tempted in an external sense and has no great struggle to do right; in the second he is tempted in the full internal sense. In both, however, he has opportunity for the practice of virtue, and, therefore, the first has all the advantage which the second has without its evils.

Thus the temptation we pray to avoid is, I suggest, that internal temptation which consists in having a strong desire for evil and which puts virtue in grave danger, while what we pray to have is such a strong tendency to good that, although external temptation may be present and the struggle may be painful, there shall be no internal temptation with grave danger of sin.

This view is supported by the following argument. Temptation in the strict sense implies a strong attraction to evil, but such a state of affairs can never be good or desirable in itself. Indeed God himself, the absolute good, can never have the slightest tendency or temptation to evil. This of course is not to deny that temptation may be an unavoidable element in human life on earth—perhaps an unavoidable element to some extent in the life of any conscious created being—but, if so, God only permits that degree of temptation which necessarily goes with human nature and with the condition of the human race which man by his free choice has brought about. Temptation is not the material out of which virtue is fashioned, but is an evil which sometimes accompanies the growth of virtue. In short, other things being equal, the less temptation the better for virtue; it is false to think that the more temptation the more chance of virtue. Grace may be given which removes temptation without lowering the value of human conduct or decreasing the power of the will, indeed which strengthens the power of the will. It may strengthen the will while taking away the power of choice. Struggle is not necessary to develop strength of will—apart from accidental circumstances—for strength of will is nothing else than a strong tendency or desire for good which God may give to a creature, if circumstances render this possible, without any conflict with evil.

Finally, we can apply these principles to the good influence which one man may have over another. If we try to persuade a man to act rightly are we not simply making things easier for him, with the result that the standard required of him is higher, whereas, if we had left him alone, the standard would have been lower, but he would have been equally free to do his best? An example of the practical importance of the problem may be seen in missionary work. If a non-Christian can act up to his lights, can even have the baptism of desire, and so be pleasing to God without explicit knowledge of Christianity, does not this take half the fervour out of mission-ary effort? The question is an important one in many spheres.

Now it is quite true that no one can do more than act up to his lights and, if he does this, he is a good man however dim his lights may be. Nevertheless, we can make it easier for other men to practise virtue, and can give them opportunities to reach a higher degree of perfection than would otherwise have been possible. If a heathen becomes a Christian he receives grace which he would not have received, if he had remained a pagan, whatever might have been his good will. We have already seen that struggle and difficulty are not essential to meritorious action, but that action can be good and meri-torious, the man's own personal act, not forced upon him by external circumstances, even if it is not the result of choice. Hence it follows that the easier we can make virtue the better, because it is more likely to be practised. One reason why we tend to think that an action is less valuable if it is made easier is that, for accidental reasons, the easier choice may not in-volve the experience that the harder choice involves, and as a result the good habit may not be so firmly established. Sometimes when it is made easier to gain fresh knowledge or skill this may mean that the knowledge or skill is not so thoroughly mastered. But under such circumstances the alternative does not really lie between making the virtue or the skill easier, and not doing so; it may be in fact impossible, for accidental reasons, to make it easier. If we could make it easier it would certainly be better to do so.

So the answer to the question seems to be this. When the missionary converts the heathen, he makes it possible for the heathen to become more perfect than he would otherwise have been. A man is not judged by the good will which he has originated, because no creature can originate virtue; it is all received from God. The more love of God that a man has, however easy it may have been for him to gain it, the more perfect he is. On the other hand a man deserves blame if he does not act up to his lights, whatever the lights may be. Consequently there is the strongest of motives for the missionary to preach to the heathen for, if the heathen listens, he will reach a higher degree of perfection, even though, if he had never heard the missionary, he might have done the best in his power.

# CHAPTER VIII

# PUNISHMENT

Punishment is the pain which is suffered deservedly on account of wrong conduct, and to discuss it we must ask whether there can be any value or purpose in pain. We have been considering God's providence and found that this led us to consider why God should permit evil. Punishment raises special questions which ought not to be passed over.

## PAIN, PURPOSELESS IN ITSELF, MAY INDIRECTLY SERVE A GOOD PURPOSE

Pain means the awareness of some desire or tendency which is frustrated. Obviously pain cannot satisfy the sufferer himself because it means frustration, and frustration is precisely what is not desired or desirable. But neither can it give ultimate satisfaction to anyone else, because this can only come from positive perfection, not from frustration. In short, pain cannot as such be good, because good is that which fulfils a purpose and satisfies a tendency or desire, while pain is by definition frustration of purpose and desire.

But, if this is so, is not the question whether there can be any value or purpose in pain settled at once? If pain is not good, surely it must be evil, and therefore valuable neither in itself nor as a means? The problem is not, however, so simple as this, for, although pain is due to frustration, it has a positive aspect; when suffering pain we are conscious of some positive power or faculty which is frustrated. Hence pain in its positive aspect, though clearly not an ultimate good, may have some causality.

We have to ask, therefore, whether pain may have a value as a means to ultimate good, and we must distinguish two senses in which this may be true. Pain may be merely the inevitable accompaniment of the process producing the good result, not a positive cause but yet unavoidable if the good result is to be gained, or the pain may itself produce the good.

Pain may be the accompaniment of good, as when it accompanies the healing of the body, or it may be itself the cause of good, as when it gives notice of approaching disease, or when it makes the sinner realize the true character of sin, and so reform himself. Pain may be a cause of virtue, of patience or unworldliness, or reliance on God, or prayer. There can be no doubt that pain may have value as a means to good in this way. Yet we should notice carefully that it can only be an indirect means to good, showing the value of good indirectly by showing the lack of value, the undesirability of evil. Pain can never directly cause good on account of its negative character, but it can do so indirectly by acting as a warning and showing that a given line of action or inaction will lead to more pain.

It is important also to notice that in both these cases, since the pain is only a means to the good or an accompaniment of it, not the good end itself, it would be better if, by some extraordinary means, the end could be reached without the pain. Pain cannot, as I have said, be valuable in itself and for its own sake; it cannot be a final end, and indeed in itself it is always undesirable, and should if possible be prevented, because it comes from frustration. Therefore, even though sometimes pain may be necessary in normal circumstances in order to gain a good end, it would be better if the circumstances could be changed. It is better to give an anaesthetic when an operation is performed, for pain in itself is never good. But may it not be conceivable that the circumstances should be changed, and the pain avoided? No doubt this may be so, but even then it remains true that the pain is no part of the good end, but in itself is undesirable.

There is no great difficulty in seeing that pain may have a value in the ways I have just been mentioning but, when we consider the question of pain suffered as punishment, we have a much harder task. What is the purpose or value of pain suffered by a sinner because he has done wrong?

It is obvious that pain may have the good purpose of making the sinner himself, and also other potential sinners, realize the need to avoid sin. In so far as punishment is reformative or preventive there is no difficulty in seeing that the pain involved in it may have value, though here again we should remember that the pain is not the final end in view, and that it would be better to avoid it if the end could be gained in a different way.

The difficulty comes when we ask whether there is any further purpose in inflicting pain on the wrongdoer, or, in other words, whether punishment should ever be retributive, and not merely reformative or preventive. Now what can be meant by retributive punishment; what other purpose can punishment have apart from reforming the sinner and preventing others from sinning? Pain cannot be an end in itself, desirable for its own sake, but, if it is only a means, how can it be a means except as a warning to show the true character of sin? We can understand that pain is able to bring home to the sinner and to others the fact that sin leads in the end to unhappiness, but can it have any other value?

## ST THOMAS'S THEORY OF PUNISHMENT

The explanation given by St Thomas is roughly as follows. Sin is committed because a man's will chooses wrongly. When a man sins he acts against reason and the divine law, and as a result his soul loses its brightness, incurring what is called metaphorically a stain (*Summa Theol.* Ia IIae, Qu. 86, art. 1, *c*). Sin offends against the three orders to which man is subject, reason, human law, and divine law, and incurs the punishment of remorse, punishment from man, and also from God (Ia IIae, Qu. 87, art. 1, *c*).

The stain of sin cannot be removed until the soul is joined again to God, and this is done through the action of the will. The stain cannot be taken away unless the sinner's will accepts the order of divine justice, which implies punishment. When the stain is removed the sinner still deserves punishment. It is true that the stain of sin is removed and the wound in the soul healed so far as the will is concerned, but punishment is still necessary to heal these other powers of the soul which were damaged by the sin, but can be cured by that which is contrary to them, namely, pain. For a sinner has transgressed the order of justice by indulging his will inordinately, and justice demands that he should suffer something against his will. That is why he deserves punishment (Ia IIae, Qu. 87, art. 6). By punishment in its strict sense "equality of justice is restored, in so far as he who by sin has followed his own will to excess suffers something against his will" (IIa, IIae, Qu. 108, art. 4, c).

Punishment is of two kinds, namely, punishment in its strict sense, and punishment of satisfaction. The first occurs when the sinner does not accept punishment willingly, while the second occurs when the sinner has repented, and accepts the punishment willingly (Ia IIae, Qu. 87, art. 7, c).

Thus St Thomas says that the special purpose of punishment is to restore the balance of justice by the infliction of pain, the amount of pain corresponding to the amount of wrong indulgence. Its purpose is, further, by setting right the balance of justice to enable the wound in the soul to be healed, which exists even when the will has been corrected.

Let us examine this theory, and first let us consider what is meant by restoring the balance of justice. What does justice mean? St Thomas says: "We should see the true justice of God in his giving to all things their due according to the worth of each existing thing, and in his keeping the nature of each thing in its proper order and power" (Ia, Qu. 21, art. 1, c). Justice, therefore, consists in giving each thing its due. It follows that, when God acts with a view to justice, as he always does, his ultimate purpose is a positive one; his aim is the positive perfection of his creatures. It is unthinkable that he should cause any frustration or pain in creatures as an end in itself, since this would be, literally, purposeless. Consequently, God brings about the order of justice by perfecting creatures positively to the extent that their natures and circumstances allow, and, implied by this, in not perfecting them beyond this point. The end in view is positive perfection, but this end involves the negative result that a creature does not receive perfection beyond its due, and suffers whatever frustration this involves. God never wills evil as such, but "he wills the evil of a natural defect or the evil of punishment by willing some good to which the evil is attached" (Ia, Qu. 19, art. 9, *c*).

What conclusion, then, are we to draw? Restoring the balance of justice, re-establishing a just order, can only mean doing what is positively good, namely restoring a right condition of affairs, while permitting the pain involved in this. The negative purpose of punishment, the permission or infliction of pain, cannot be detached from the positive purpose, if justice is the aim; the infliction of pain cannot be regarded as a separate purpose with a value in itself. God aims at the positive perfection of his creatures, and permits pain only because positive perfection requires this. An action which aimed at nothing more than the infliction of pain, even when deserved, would not be a just action, and could not have the effect of bringing about a just order, because the bringing about of a just order implies the giving of positive perfection. Therefore, punishment, even when justly inflicted, can never be an end in itself; it can only be a means for re-establishing positive good, or a necessary accompaniment of this. Punishment is retributive in the sense that it is deserved by the sinner, but it is not merely retrospective but rather prospective, aiming, through pain, at bringing about a positive perfection.

Can we accept the theory that the purpose of punishment is to balance a wrong satisfaction by corresponding pain? Two difficulties may be suggested against it. First, there is the difficulty that something can be taken away only if it is still

there to take away, and, if the wrong satisfaction is past, there
appears to be nothing to take away so as to restore the balance
of justice. Secondly, how can pain put right the wrong situation
in the sinner? It is the pain as such which is said to balance the
wrong indulgence and correct the state of the sinner, but pain
is awareness of frustration and cannot, surely, cause any
positive good. Pain can give warning of evil simply because it
is pain, but it cannot of itself do positive good. It is very hard
to see how frustration, which is negative, can possibly cure
the wound in the soul and restore positive perfection.

However, if we are unable to accept this part of St Thomas's
theory, it does not follow that we cannot accept the rest. We
can agree that sin not only implies that the will is turned away
from God, but also that the other powers of the soul are
wounded and damaged. Hence we can agree that punishment,
often at least, is concerned with healing the soul as well as
with converting the will. When the doctor heals the body pain
is only incidental and is not the cause of the healing, although
excessive indulgence may have deserved the pain which accompanies the healing. So too with punishment. Of course God
may inflict punishment also to make the sinner repent, or to
deter others from sin, but this raises no difficult problem. God
may also permit the sinner to suffer pain because this is inevitable if certain good ends are to be realized. The question
is whether punishment has any other purpose, and the conclusion, I suggest, is that it has not. Undoubtedly punishment
re-establishes the just order, but this only means that positive
good is brought about even when this involves that the sinner
shall suffer pain which he deserves to suffer.

We must consider some objections against this view. Surely,
it may be said, it is wrong that a sinner should profit from his
sin, as would happen if he enjoyed a wrong satisfaction without any corresponding pain. And does not this imply that it is
a good action with a good purpose if we set the situation right
by inflicting punishment? Need we look for any further
justification beyond the fact that the pain is deserved? If

punishment ought not to be inflicted for its own sake, would it not be wrong to punish the incorrigible sinner?

It is certainly wrong that a sinner should profit by his sin, and we must presume that in the end the natural consequence of sin will be pain. But the question is whether it would be a good action to anticipate these normal consequences, and inflict punishment now. If this is necessary to put right the results of sin, clearly the punishment should be inflicted, since undoubtedly the sinner deserves whatever pain is required to put right the effects of his sin, and to prevent him from doing further harm. But, if no good purpose could be achieved for anyone by his punishment, if no positive perfection at all would result, then, if it is not at the moment inevitable, it seems useless and therefore wrong to inflict it. There seems no good purpose in causing pain, even when it is deserved, if there is no other reason than that it is deserved. When we say pain is deserved surely we only mean it ought to be inflicted, if some positive good will be gained by so doing.

This at once brings up the question: Can we suppose that punishment for wrongdoing is in the end inevitable, that it does not in itself have any purpose, but is only an accompaniment of the process of good in the universe? If this is so the pain of such punishment would not necessarily be the pain involved in the process of healing; it would be simply the pain resulting from violation of the laws of the universe. It would have no purpose in itself, and could only be the accompaniment of good, not necessarily in the sinner himself, but in others. We should have to say that God permits the sinner to suffer pain because this is involved in his plan for the good of his creation, a wrong use of free choice making pain follow as a necessary consequence.

## PUNISHMENT AND MERCY

It seems quite reasonable to think that this may be true, but it would not of course mean that the other kinds of punishment

were not justifiable. There is, however, an important proviso
to bear in mind. Punishment cannot be wholly unavoidable,
for all agree that God can show mercy, and modify the punishment that might be otherwise unavoidable. God can certainly
forgive the repentant sinner, and can even mitigate the punishment of the sinner who is not repentant.

This raises an obvious problem: does not mercy contradict
justice? If mercy is better than justice, why must God sometimes show justice; why does he not always show mercy instead
of justice, where punishment is concerned? Does not justice
demand mercy?

St Thomas tells us that God does not act against justice
when he acts mercifully; he gives more than he need, and remits
what is owing to him (Ia, Qu. 21, art. 3, ad 2). But how can
God give more than he need, and remit what is owing to him,
when he need not even give being to the creature, and when
all that the creature possesses is received from God? Nothing
that happens to the creature affects God in himself at all.

Now we have seen that justice means giving what is due,
what a creature requires and is capable of receiving for its
perfection. What is just for the creature depends, therefore, on
the powers given him by God. Thus God acts justly when he
permits the creature to suffer pain, if pains follow as a result
of sin, because sin has damaged the creature's powers. But
how, then, can God show mercy and relieve the pain? This
seems possible if God does not merely act in accordance with
the creature's powers as they have already been given him, but
goes further and gives greater powers beyond these. God is
not bound in justice to add supernatural powers to man's
natural powers, but he has done so. Justice consists in giving
what the creature has the capacity to receive, while mercy consists in giving more than this. If the creature sins, even though
he repents, his healing, we may suppose, would be slow and
painful in the normal course. God, however, may give further
powers and heal the sinner rapidly and without pain, and thus
may go beyond justice and show mercy by remitting punishment.

But why, then, does not God always go beyond justice, if mercy is better? The reply is sometimes made that God must show both mercy and justice, and that, if he were always merciful, there would be a failure in justice. This, however, does not seem to follow. To be merciful is not to fail in justice, for justice is giving what is due, while mercy is giving more than what is due. There is, therefore, no reason on this score why God should not always be merciful. The only reason that seems satisfactory is the same as I have given to explain why God permits evil, namely, that the apparently more merciful course would not really be more merciful. We must suppose that the highest and ultimate interests of the human race as a whole would not be advanced, if God showed more mercy. We should remember, however, that we shall not know the full extent of God's mercy until the end of the world; we may know what justice requires, but we do not know all that God's mercy may do, because it is not yet revealed.

The following point should be added to forestall an objection. There is no question of God's changing his plan, or adding anything as an afterthought. God's plan is determined upon in its entirety from eternity, but there are, so to speak, stages in it which, though foreseen from the beginning, are distinct. In the first stage God gives certain powers, and in the second God gives further powers, and he may give still other powers. Thus what is just in relation to the second stage is merciful in relation to the first stage. Mercy and justice depend for their meaning on the particular powers to which we refer. Moreover all that God gives he gives out of mercy in the sense that nothing is owing to the creature, while all that God gives is given out of justice in the sense that God intends to realize his purpose. To apply this to punishment, sin which in the first stage of God's plan may require much suffering before its effects can be put right, may in the second stage be healed more easily. Hence punishment, which is inevitable under the conditions of the first stage, may be mitigated under the conditions of the second.

## CONCLUSIONS ABOUT PUNISHMENT

Let us take stock of the situation at this point. The conclusions reached about punishment are roughly these. Just punishment is the pain which a sinner suffers either simply as a result of his sin, or in order to put right its effects. Thus the reasons for punishment may be very various. For example the reason may be:

1. That the pain is necessary to correct the sinner's will.

2. That the pain is necessary for the healing of the soul's other powers damaged by sin.

3. That the pain is necessary to put right any wrong effects upon other people.

4. That the pain is necessary for restraining the sinner from further sin.

5. That the pain is necessary for the good of other people, although no good can result to the sinner because he is unrepentant.

Further, the following points seem clear:

1. The pain of punishment is never desirable in itself, and, if the purpose could be gained without the pain, this would be better.

2. To inflict punishment, if it is not a means to, or a necessary accompaniment of, positive good, would be purposeless and wrong.

3. The establishment of the just order means giving everything the positive perfection due to it, and, with a view to this, in permitting or inflicting any pain needed to put right the effects of the sin.

4. It is difficult to see why corresponding pain should be necessary in justice to balance wrong satisfaction, except in the sense that sin may be expected in the end to incur corresponding pain.

5. God may show mercy in some circumstances, and bring about the good purpose which would otherwise be accom-

panied by, or caused by, the pain of punishment, without the sinner suffering this pain.

Punishment, then, presents a very complex problem. The pain of punishment may have a purpose for the sinner in so far as it indirectly serves to promote some good, for example, by making the sinner realize the value of good by realizing the character of evil, or it may have no purpose for the sinner, but simply be the inevitable result of wrongdoing. It may be unavoidable, or it may be avoidable, though necessary for the good of the sinner or of others affected by the sinner's act. The sinner may be repentant or unrepentant, and this may affect the purpose of punishment. Punishment may be inflicted by man or God, and be different for this reason. Therefore, if the question is asked, what is the purpose of punishment, the answer will vary widely. The feature common to all punishment seems only to be that it is pain which results from sin, and is deserved by the sinner because he is responsible for the consequences of his sin.

Now the object of this chapter is to see how punishment can form a part of God's providential plan. It will be useful, therefore, to apply very briefly in a number of different spheres the conclusions just reached.

## APPLICATIONS OF THESE CONCLUSIONS

First, let us take punishment in the present life, and we must distinguish between man's punishments and God's punishments. Man's punishments may be of course reformative or preventive. Such punishments do not heal the sinner directly, but do so indirectly by making sin painful. Again, if the sinner is unrepentant, punishment may also have the object of restraining him from further evil. God's punishment in this life may have the same aims as those of man, but in addition God may heal the soul of the repentant sinner, and pain may accompany this.

Then comes the punishment of purgatory. There is no

question here of correcting the will, since it is now finally
determined upon good. Therefore, it seems that the punishment must be the pain accompanying the healing of these
powers in the soul which have been damaged by the will's
choice of evil.

The punishment of hell raises greater difficulties. Can we say
that its purpose is to manifest God's justice? We have seen that
the primary purpose of justice is to give each creature the
positive perfection it deserves and is capable of. The purpose
of justice for the damned must be the negative purpose of
withholding the perfection they were originally capable of, and
allowing the frustration resulting from their sins. The question
is how the manifestation of this negative side of justice can
promote any positive good. It may be suggested that it shows
God's power to overcome evil. But it is difficult to see how the
realization by the blessed that sin leads to punishment can be
a source of positive perfection. The overcoming of evil by
turning it to good is of course a source of joy, but it is hard to
see how the spectacle of evil unrepentant, though punished,
that is to say, of the negative side of God's justice, can be a
source of joy.

It seems more plausible to say that the punishment of the
damned is the inevitable result of violation of the laws of the
universe, which God plans for the good of creatures. This
explanation, however, also presents difficulties. Can God be
forced to keep the damned in being in the state of damnation?
If it is replied that this is necessary for the good of the saved,
why should it be necessary after the last judgement? Moreover
it is held by theologians, including St Thomas, that God's
mercy is such that even the punishment of hell is mitigated
(Ia, Qu. 21, art. 4, ad 1), and, if this is so, it cannot be absolutely inevitable. Can we say that it is inevitable in the normal
course of events, and when the laws of the universe work out
to their natural result, but that, nevertheless, God can, in his
mercy, bring higher powers to bear, and override the normal
laws? This, however, again leads to the question: Is there any

limit to the power of God's mercy; is he only able to mitigate the punishment in some small degree and no more? If the punishment is not absolutely inevitable it is hard to see where we must stop. What principle makes it inevitable up to a certain point and no further? The answer perhaps is that we simply do not know what mercy God will show.

Another possible reason for punishment in hell might be to restrain the damned from further sin, but the difficulty against this is that the essential punishment of the damned is the pain of loss, and the pain of loss is not aimed at their restraint. Another reason might be to keep others from a similar fate, the purpose of deterrence. St Thomas says: "Even the eternal punishments of the damned inflicted by God are medicinal to those who abstain from sin out of consideration of the punishments" (Ia IIae, Qu. 87, art. 3, ad 2). However, the punishment of hell cannot surely be fully explained as a deterrent. Nor would it help if we admitted that a wrong indulgence must always have a corresponding pain, for what positive good would this serve either to the damned or to the saved?

Another question concerns the purpose of punishment inflicted by the sinner upon himself as a penance, or accepted willingly from another, during the present life. Here we have a situation in which the sinner is repentant and causes pain to himself, or accepts it, but in which the pain is not inevitable, and is not the necessary accompaniment of any process of healing. What reason can there be for this? The most obvious explanation seems to be that, when a man repents of a sin, he wishes not only to put right any harm he has done, but also to impress on his memory the need to avoid sin in the future. The pain he inflicts on himself has this object, and it also raises a barrier against sin by connecting it with pain. In addition there is no doubt an instinctive desire to show repentance by showing a willingness to suffer pain. If one man has harmed another and is sorry for doing so, he may wish to show his sorrow by his readiness to suffer in order to put the matter right. The pain has not any value in itself, but is just a sign of repentance and desire to make any restitution that is required. Thus pain suffered as a penance may have the purpose of emphasizing the need to avoid sin, or of giving a good example of hatred of sin, and so of preventing scandal, and in these ways may be an act of justice. Yet the pain is no more than an indirect means to good, and has no value in itself. It can only be right to make use of pain in moderation, to prevent greater evil.

Apart, however, from the purpose of punishment for personal sin, there may be another reason for self-inflicted pain. It may be needed for the development of self-control, which is perhaps the immediate object of asceticism. The need for this, though due as such to no personal fault, is the result of original sin and of the disorder in man's desires which this has caused. St Paul expresses its purpose when he says: "I buffet my own body, and make it my slave" (1 Cor. 9. 27). Hence the reason for pain inflicted as training is much the same as the reason for punishment, but in the former case it is not the result of the person's own sin, as it is in the latter case. We should notice that, since the aim is self-control, it would be quite false to think that the more pain a man inflicts on himself the better he is. There is a definite object in view, and only that amount and kind of pain is right which is likely to further the end. Too much pain, and pain of a wrong kind, would make self-control harder rather than easier, and indeed lack of reasonable pleasure and satisfaction would do the same. The right amount of pain must depend on the character and circumstances of a particular person, and this negative aim should not be allowed to interfere with the positive human activities, which are the important object. Moreover, if self-control could be gained without painful restraint, then painful restraint would have no purpose. The pain is only a means to the end, and it is a means which in itself is undesirable.

It may be asked how, if pain is undesirable and as such against God's will, it can be inflicted as a means to reform or self-control. It should be remembered, however, that sin deserves whatever pain is necessary to put right its effects, or, better, that the effects of sin should be put right, even though the sinner has to suffer the evil of pain in putting them right. For this reason it is right that pain should be inflicted as a penance for sin, if this will help to correct the sinner. Similarly, it is right that pain should be suffered in the attempt to develop self-control, in so far as the need for this is due to sin. But there is also the more general principle that it is better to gain a great good even though evil of certain kinds is involved than not to gain this good. God permits evil in the world, because it is better to do this and gain the good he desires than not to gain it.

Let us turn to another aspect of the question, and ask whether, granting the truth of what I have been saying, punishment for sin can be borne by someone other than the sinner himself. Can one man be punished justly instead of another? If we take punishment to mean pain deserved by a sinner because of his sin, plainly no one but the sinner can be punished justly, because no one else deserves it. Punishment is just, because it is due to the sinner on account of his choice of evil. St Thomas says: "If we speak of punishment precisely as such, then it is always related to a man's own fault" (Ia IIae, Qu. 87, art. 7). This is the fundamental principle, but there is more to be said. An innocent man may suffer as the result of another's sin, and in a sense be punished, though unjustly, for it. Moreover, it is possible that another man may be willing to suffer pain in order to relieve a sinner of the pain of his just punishment.

How can a sinner be relieved in this way? We have seen that punishment, if it is just, is a necessary accompaniment of some positively good end, or a means to gain it. Plainly, therefore, it would not be right to relieve the sinner of the pain due to him, if this involved a loss of perfection either to the sinner or to someone else to whom it was due. But this is not always the case. In the natural order, if a man gets ill through self-indulgence the doctor may rightly cure him without pain, even though the illness is a just punishment. The question is: if we look at the matter from the point of view of ultimate justice, is it conceivable that a sinner should ever be relieved of his punishment through the efforts of someone else, so that he need never suffer the pain he deserves on account of his sin?

We must keep in mind that the pain of punishment is not desirable in itself, but only for the sake of some positively good end. A man ought to be punished if this is necessary to put right the effects of his sin, but not when this condition is not fulfilled. Therefore, if the good end can be gained through the efforts of someone else, without pain to the sinner, no wrong is done. The pain in itself is undesirable and, if someone else, at cost to himself, is willing to prevent it, this is a good act, done out of charity, achieving a situation in which perfection is gained and none lost. There does not seem any reason to think justice demands that a sinner, when repentant, must necessarily himself suffer pain, because he has sinned. Pain is only the negative side of justice and, if the positive perfection of creatures can, in spite of sin, be gained without pain, then justice is done, and it is better so. This gives an explanation of the power of God to remit the punishment due to the repentant sinner without any infringement of justice.

Above all it is important to remember that, if one man's punishment is relieved by another, this does not mean that the latter's pain is substituted for the former's, as though pain were a sum of money which was owed, and which could be paid by one man on behalf of another. The idea of debt may be used metaphorically of punishment, but not literally. Pain is frustration, and not a positive entity, and it would be absurd to speak of substituting pain for pain in a literal sense; pain cannot of itself directly benefit any one. What is right is that one man should be willing to suffer pain because this is unavoidable if he is to save the other man from the pain which would normally result from his sin. Certainly it is unthinkable that God should desire pain in any creature, except in so far as it is necessary for some positive good; pain as such can never be pleasing to God. We sometimes find it said that God demands victims willing to suffer, almost as though he requires a given quantity of pain, no matter who suffers it, and when the pain is not necessary for positive perfection. But God can only require victims in the sense of requiring creatures willing to do a good act in spite of the pain involved. Pain is only an unfortunate necessity, to be endured for the sake of gaining positive perfection.

Whether the person who relieves the pain of another's punishment suffers himself in doing so does not affect the justice or the efficacy of his act. If, however, suffering is unavoidable for this end, and someone else endures it for the sake of the sinner, plainly this is an act of great love and highest virtue.

Finally, it is sometimes thought that, since the pain suffered by the Christian enables him to share in Christ's redemptive act, therefore the more pain suffered for this end the better. No doubt this is perfectly true in the sense that, provided the pain is necessary for some good purpose, it is God's will that it should be suffered, and it can be used as an occasion for sharing in Christ's redemptive act. But it is not true that we ought to cause ourselves pain, quite dissociated from any good end, for this purpose. Pain could not be willed by God for its own sake, when not required for positive perfection, and it is only when this condition is fulfilled that pain can be made use of for union with Christ.

These remarks will be sufficient, I hope, to give some idea of the kind of value pain can have and, therefore, of the value of punishment. We can see that pain and punishment may have a purpose in God's providential plan.

# CHAPTER IX

# CONCLUSIONS

## *SUMMARY OF THE ARGUMENT*

It will be well to take a glance backwards over the argument, and look at it as a whole. I started by arguing that man has the power of free choice, and the question is how God's loving providence can govern all things if there is evil in creation, and if some creatures have free choice and can do evil.

Why does God allow evil in creation? God is almighty in the sense that he can do all that is conceivable, but yet what it is conceivable that God should do in perfecting his creatures is in some ways limited. The reason I have suggested why God permits evil in creation is that it is unavoidable if supreme perfection is to be ultimately possible. There is no absolute necessity for God to permit evil, for there is no absolute necessity for him to create. It is contradictory and meaningless, however, that God should not permit evil, granted that creatures are to exist as they do exist.

Some evil, therefore, can be accounted for as inevitable in God's plan. On the other hand, some evil may be explained as due to the creature's free choice, and as contrary to God's plan. How can we explain free choice? I have argued that it consists in seeking either a greater or a lesser good. If we choose the greater good we do not originate any activity, but simply act up to the full capacity of which we are capable, moved to this by God. Our action is then fully accounted for by the causes which act upon us. If we choose the lesser good we fail to do all that we are capable of doing, and the failure originates in ourselves, and has no further cause. Free choice is not a power which as such has value for human perfection, but under certain conditions it is inevitable if there is to be the possibility of ultimate, supreme, perfection. The result of free choice may be a violation of God's plan, and this leads to pain, and to the punishment of the sinner.

We come, then, to the crucial problem, which is the problem of God's predestination of his creatures. This word has of course been a battle ground for theological disputes. The sense in which I am using it here is to express God's determination in every detail from eternity of every event in creation. Everything in creation comes from God, depends on God, and is determined by God. The reason for saying this is that we are speaking of creature and creator, of effect and total cause. But how are we to explain the fact that violations of God's plan occur?

It is essential to keep firmly in mind that God sees everything from eternity, though creation works itself out subject to succession. There is no question of foreknowledge in God, because he sees everything simultaneously with its happening, and more than this, from the standpoint of eternity. There is causal order in creation as God sees it, but he sees temporal events from outside time. This being so we can express God's providence as follows. He sees the thing he wills to create with its perfections and with the limitations imposed by its nature and by the free choice of its individuals, and he gives it being accordingly. He permits the natural limitations and frustrations, he permits the use of free choice, and he permits all this because it is inevitable if the good is to be achieved which he desires. There is no contradiction in saying that he permits free choice, because the creature does not initiate positive action when he chooses; if the creature fails he only initiates failure, which as such is negative. God limits the causal activity he exercises in creation, in accordance with these conditions, which he sees from eternity.

## PREDESTINATION

Now let us put this in terms of predestination. God predestines every man from eternity to every event that happens to him, because it is all brought about by God's causality. If a man is to gain heaven, God predestines him to all the graces he receives, to his supernatural state, and to eternal glory. God causes him to gain merit through his good actions, and God rewards these merits which he himself has caused. Even though they are received from God they deserve their reward, for they spring from the kind of conduct which is designed to lead to further perfection. On the other hand God predestines those who sin to the state of punishment which they deserve, if this follows inevitably from their failure, that is, if they do not repent and gain forgiveness. Their failure is due to themselves alone, and is permitted by God, because human personality must be allowed full play if the highest good is to be possible.

On some such lines as these I suggest that we may reach a theory which throws light on the difficult problem and avoids contradiction. I will mention a few further points which may help to bring out its meaning.

If choice depends on a conflict of desires, why, it may be said, cannot God strengthen the creature's desire for good to such an extent that in fact wrong desires will never prevail? To this question it is surely reasonable to reply that in the present life we see only a small part of God's design for creation. The design is presumably highly complex, and the parts interconnected in ways that we cannot follow. There may, therefore, be reasons unknown to us which make it inconceivable that God should strengthen to such an extent the creature's desire for good. But, apart from this general argument, we can see a possible line of explanation. For, if the creature can only be perfected by a gradual process, the supreme attraction of the final end may at the beginning of the process be necessarily obscure. It may be impossible at this stage, at least normally, for the creature to have such a clear perception of the attractiveness of good as would ensure right conduct.

The difficulty, however, may be pressed. Even granting the truth of what has just been said it may seem hard to believe that more help could not often be given than in fact is given.

Is not man in this world so weak and ignorant that a right choice is sometimes almost beyond his power? Should we not at least expect that right conduct would be less difficult than it often is?

Now Christian doctrine helps us to meet this difficulty, for it teaches us that the present state of the human race has been brought about by sins committed in the past, by the fall of some of the angels and by the fall of man. The answer, then, to the question why there is so much difficulty in doing right is that in the first place this was not so, but that sin has brought it about.

Therefore, when we reflect on the evils of the present world, we must remember that, according to Christian teaching, God permitted originally in his plan only so much evil as was inevitable apart from sin. God permitted some of his creatures to have the power of free choice, because this was inevitable if supreme perfection was to be possible, and as a result of wrong choice other evils have mounted up. Consequently, when the question is asked: "Why has God put us in such conditions as he has?", we can reply that the present conditions are not in accordance with God's original plan. In the first place God set men in paradise. We must remember, too, that even now he offers us, when this life is over, a happiness beyond our powers of conception.

It follows that there is a sense in which this is the best of possible worlds and a sense in which it is not. Here and now it is far from being the best because sin has damaged it, while, even apart from this, this life would have been only an opening phase in our progress towards perfection. On the other hand even under present conditions we have the hope of reaching in the end the state of supreme happiness and perfection in the beatific vision, and from this point of view no life could be better.

## THE QUESTION OF MIRACLES

In connection with this question of the difficulty of right

choice a word should be said about miracles. Why cannot God work more miracles than he does, and thus ensure that man will overwhelmingly desire the good? We must suppose, however, that God's design for the world would be spoiled if he intervened, except rarely, by working miracles. God's plan seems to be based on certain general laws whose effect is to produce the kind of result intended. To alter these profoundly or continuously would be to alter the plan and its results essentially; it would be a contradiction of God's intention. As to how miracles can have a place in God's providence, in view of the fact that all is predestined from eternity we shall have to say this. A miracle is an event of a startling character, which is usually intended to produce a special effect on those who witness it. Therefore some miracles may occur because the original state of things at creation was so planned that by the ordinary laws of causality certain striking events would occur at appropriate moments. If this is so a miracle would not necessarily imply any abnormal causality, but it would be the result of God's original design at creation. There are other miracles, however, which are due to a special causal act on God's part which overrides the normal sequence of cause and effect in human affairs. Such miracles must also of course have been foreordained from eternity, and the normal chain of cause and effect adjusted accordingly.

## THE RIGHT ATTITUDE TO GOD'S PROVIDENCE

Let us turn now to another side of this question of God's providence, and consider the way in which in the present life men should regard it. How should it affect their outlook? What are the implications of belief in God's loving providence as here explained?

To begin with it implies that God will bring all men, who act rightly and repent their sins, with absolute certainty to eternal happiness. That is the essential fact about God's providence, and it means that we can have complete confidence in

God's love of us and in God's power to bring about our salvation. St Augustine says that God would never allow evil in creation, unless he was so almighty and so good that out of evil he could bring good. This must be so for men of good will, because God desires the salvation of all, and it would be contradictory to suppose that he would allow this intention to be thwarted finally except through the individual's own fault. Thus, if a man does right he knows for certain that, whatever he may suffer either because it is inevitable or because it has been caused by another man's sin, this can never do him ultimate harm, and that the final good will abundantly compensate for all passing evil. External causes can never of themselves affect a man's good will and so do him ultimate harm; he can only fail in a way that will affect his final destiny through his own fault, that is, when he is capable of not failing. If external forces, over which he has no control, increase his desire for wrong beyond a certain point, or lessen his desire for good beyond a certain point, he ceases to be capable of doing right, and ceases to be responsible for doing wrong. Choice is only possible when there is a conflict of desires, which means when the desire for either good or evil is strong enough to form a motive which he can follow. Provided, therefore, that a man does not do wrong when he is capable of doing right, that is, provided he does not sin, he can have complete confidence that God's providence will lead him to ultimate perfection and happiness.

On the other hand there does not seem any reason to think that God will necessarily bring good out of evil in the natural order in this world. Certainly the evidence seems to show that in the universe as we know it in the present life natural forces follow their laws without special intervention of God's providence, except occasionally and for particular purposes, and that human affairs depend for the most part on man's free choice and the laws of human nature. There may be periods when human well-being will go forward, but Christian teaching gives us no assurance about such things. Indeed Christian teaching, though it tells us to work for human good in this life, only promises that these efforts will be successful in the life to come. We are taught that original sin has left man open to the effects of sin in this world. Thus God has his providential plan in every sphere, in that of grace, in that of physical law, in that of human history. The only question is how far the plan is upset by sin. We can only say that God lets the cockle grow with the good seed, because more harm than good would be done by tearing it up, that he always has a providential plan for human affairs even though (to speak from our point of view) it has to be constantly modified as a result of sin. To what extent particular events are due to special intervention we cannot usually know.

Our attitude, therefore, to God's providence should be one of trust and resignation. It should be one of trust because it will certainly bring us to final happiness, unless we choose to fail. It should be one of resignation because it may allow us to suffer before the end is reached. But this makes us ask the question whether the way of providence is always the most direct way to the end. Have we the comforting assurance that the troubles we meet are inevitable, and that on the whole we could not reach heaven more quickly? This is a more complicated question. We must distinguish between God's positive will and God's permissive will. Suppose, for example, a man is in a concentration camp through no fault of his own but through the sins of others. Such a situation is contrary to God's plan, and we can only say that God permits it without willing it, and that no ultimate harm will come to the innocent. Similarly if, through his own fault a man is in prison, this too is due to God's permissive will and not his positive will, because the sin and its results were not part of God's original plan. Nevertheless there is a wide difference between these two situations. In the first the sufferer, being innocent, is within the scope of God's plan for his salvation. It is true that the situation is permitted and not willed by God and that it is contrary to God's original plan. Yet, however much this may be so, when a man is innocent, or when he repents after sin, he can be sure that providence has a fresh plan to suit the new situation, and that this plan is the best for him in the circumstances. If, however, a man through his own fault is in a situation not willed by God, then plainly he is not within God's plan in any sense, unless he repents. The situation is not according to God's plan, and the man himself has put himself outside any plan of God for his good.

Thus we cannot say that every situation with which we are confronted is God's will and God's providence, and that all we have to do is to accept it. It may be only the result of God's permissive will, because it is due to sin, either our own or that of others. It may be a situation which we should do our best to change. We only ought to "abandon" ourselves to divine providence, that is to say, to accept the situation as it is and make no effort to change it, if it is a situation willed by God as his plan, or a situation which, though only permitted by God, is entirely outside our control. Then we can only be resigned to it. But we can be sure that, even though a situation is due to our own fault or that of another person, and is against God's original plan, nevertheless once we intend to do right again, divine providence will take us in the most direct way possible in the new circumstances to ultimate perfection. A situation can always be made part of God's plan again, part, that is, of a new plan which takes account of the sin committed.

We can picture it in this way. God has an original plan, which would have been carried out had no sin ever occurred. God permits sin for the reasons I have given. As each sin occurs, God adjusts his plan so as to lead men in the best way to ultimate perfection now that the sin has occurred. Of course this is an inaccurate way of putting it, because there can be no change in God; he sees from eternity the sins that will be committed, and his plan is adjusted to take account of this from eternity. Yet it is helpful to ask what would have been the plan had no sin occurred, although this plan was never in fact to be carried out.

## PRAYER AND PROVIDENCE

Here the subject of prayer comes up: how does prayer work into the scheme of divine providence; is not prayer of its very nature an attempt to change the course of events as previously planned?

St Thomas tells us that, when God is said to hear a prayer, this does not mean that God changes his intention, since God cannot change, but it means that we make ourselves capable by our prayer of receiving what God has willed from eternity to give us (IIa, IIae, Qu. 83, art. 2, *c*). God has determined from eternity that we should be moved to pray on a given occasion, and he has determined from eternity that as a result of prayer we should become capable of receiving, and should in fact receive, what we pray for. The problem is, therefore, not so much how our prayers can be heard, as how we can fail to pray when we ought to pray, and consequently how we can fail to receive what we ought to receive. There is a problem of evil, but not of good. The answer is to repeat what I have said about free choice. I have suggested that the failure is due to ourselves alone, that it is permitted by God, and that God, having seen from eternity that it would occur, has ordained things accordingly. He has permitted that we, by our failure, should lessen his causal act upon creation. The failure to pray, and to make ourselves capable of receiving the answer to our prayer, is our own responsibility.

## FREEDOM

I should like in conclusion to return to the subject of freedom, for it may seem that freedom has not been valued as it should be in these pages. This is very far from being my intention. Opinions may, however, differ as to what kind of freedom is really important. I am suggesting that the kind of freedom which is really important is freedom to realize our powers in the highest degree and to the fullest extent. Whether we can make a choice or not does not, in itself, seem to matter, provided that we can do what in the best sense we want to do. For, if I have been right in arguing that choice always lies between a desire for greater and a desire for lesser good, then it must be better for us to have only a desire for what is greater, and to be unable to fail.

Now, if this is so, and if the most important kind of freedom lies in the lack of obstacles to the fulfilment of our powers, the really important things are the powers themselves. It is because human powers are so tremendous that freedom for them is such an important matter. We should reflect, then, on our human powers and their implications, if we wish to appreciate the value of true freedom. Powers may be limited either by their natural limitations, or by external causes which prevent them from acting as they should. Our physical powers as human beings are of course actually limited, and our intellectual powers are also limited in some respects. Nevertheless, there is one way in which our intellectual powers are not limited, for we have an obscure awareness of God as the source of all things. Thus we can make God's will the motive of our conduct. Now it is precisely through this awareness of the infinite that, as I am suggesting, our power to choose arises: no limited object can satisfy our desires completely, and force us to act, for our awareness of the infinite gives us a desire to be united with it. When we possess the beatific vision and see God face to face we shall be unable as I have already said, to choose anything that opposes his will, because we shall have no such desire. Here on earth we are aware of God only dimly, and limited things have a certain immediate appeal.

It follows, then, from this that man has inherent in him a freedom of the highest kind, for he is free from compulsion by limited things. Lesser creatures can be forced to act by limited things, because they desire nothing more. Man can only be fully satisfied by the infinite. We have to remember too that man's natural freedom has been emphasized and crowned by the supernatural powers conferred by grace, making him capable in the end of seeing God face to face.

On the other hand this sublime degree of freedom which man possesses is incomplete in the present life because our awareness of the infinite is at present obscure and precarious. We can only keep the infinite in mind by an effort, and can easily let our attention slip away, and think of finite things. Thus our freedom from the compulsion of limited things is only maintained with difficulty, and we may quickly become their slaves. It comes to this: man's purpose in this life is to struggle to maintain his freedom from the compulsion of limited things, and his freedom to develop his power to seek the infinite. That is surely the important kind of freedom for human beings, and not freedom to choose.

We can better appreciate what this implies if we realize that to maintain this important kind of freedom is the same as to develop human personality. As I said earlier, it is often thought that personality is only expressed through choice, and that a man who could not choose would be a machine and not fully a man. This I suggest is not so. When we call someone a person we mean that he is a centre of activity, an agent, with intellectual and spiritual powers. A man realizes his personality the more fully he uses his highest powers. He is not realizing his personality when he uses his lower powers only, or when the action he performs is not consciously and deliberately his own, or when he is not aware of its scope and purpose as compared with other possible acts, in short, when he is not fully the agent, but is little more than an instrument through which other agents act. Of course each person is only one among many, and the individual personality is not expressed less freely because others must be taken into account. It is indeed only in and through society that the individual personality can be expressed at all.

To act, then, as a person is the proper way for a human being to act, and is of supreme value. But to act fully as a person is to act with complete freedom, because it means that we are using our powers, which in themselves are in some sense free from limitation, without any hindrance. Man can have this freedom, which is of supreme value, and yet at the same time be entirely dependent on God. For God, being absolutely and eternally unlimited, can give to his creatures the power for unlimited progress in perfection, which comes from a desire that the finite can never satisfy.

It is not a limitation to this freedom that man is entirely dependent on God. We must bear in mind that the kind of causality which God exercises is very different from the kind of causality that we exercise. We can make changes in the things around us, but we cannot create these things. We cannot maintain in being a material thing, much less a living person. God can keep in being an intellectual and spiritual being, conscious of himself and others. It is true, as I have argued, that, when man struggles to maintain his freedom from finite things, it is God's causality which struggles in him, and that only his failure to struggle is due to himself. Nevertheless it is the man himself who struggles. There is no question of God's moving a puppet; God keeps in being a conscious person, whose acts are his own acts and not God's acts. God causes the acts, but God does not himself do the acts; the creature is not a mere instrument of God, but is a person kept in being by God. That is why a creature can deserve a reward for his virtues, even though they are exercised in dependence on God. That is why, too, a creature can be responsible for its failure.

Thus man can be, and should be, and ought to be treated as, free in the sense in which freedom is most important, and yet at the same time all that he does is determined from eternity by God's providence. There is no contradiction, if my argument is sound, between God's predestination, and providential government, of man and man's freedom to realize his personality to the full, provided we understand what freedom and personality mean.

# EPILOGUE

*Question.* You have discussed the meaning of freedom and human personality in relation to God's providence, and have explained what you think is the really important kind of freedom. But can you apply this to more directly practical things? Can you show what conclusion your view would lead to with regard to the freedom an individual should have in society? To take an example, would it not mean that an individual always had a right to express his honest opinion, and that no one had a right to stop him?

*Answer.* I don't think that what I have said throws any very special light on such questions, but of course they are important in connection with freedom. It is true I have argued that a human person should be free to use his powers to the full, and should therefore not be a mere instrument in the hands of others—that he should form his own personal judgement, as a result of his own personal reflection, on important matters. But everyone would presumably agree to this. I don't know that such a principle can decide the question of a man's right to express his opinion in order to influence his fellow men.

*Q.* It seems to imply that a man only realizes his powers as a human person to the full, if he makes up his own mind independently on important questions. But doesn't this mean that he has a right to make up his mind independently, and isn't public expression the natural outcome of private conviction?

*A.* It seems to me that a good many distinctions must be made before these questions can be answered. But to begin with I should say that no one can have a right to think or say what is false. If you have a right to do something, it must be right for you to do it; you cannot have a right to do what is wrong. So a man can only have a right, strictly speaking, to think and say what is true.

*Q*. That is obviously true, but not, I suggest, very relevant. Hasn't everyone a right to be treated as a human person, and doesn't this imply that he has a right not to be interfered with, when he forms and expresses his opinions? Of course other people who disagree should try to persuade him and convince him by argument, but surely they should not use force in any way?

*A*. That is to oversimplify. Men are not isolated individuals; they can only realize their powers as individuals in and through the society of other men. If they express their opinions outwardly they immediately begin to influence others. If contradictory influences are at work, and if they affect the vital structure of a society, in the end such a struggle may take place that the society may be broken up. Therefore complete freedom of expression may lead to the break-up of the society, through which alone the individual can realize his powers.

*Q*. Isn't this rather too theoretical an argument? In practice may we not suppose that, if people are left free to express their opinions, they will do so without violence, and that by a natural process society will get along without a break-up? Is not this the best way to ensure the permanence of a society?

*A*. I entirely agree that it is much better if everybody can be left free to express his opinions, and if in spite of this society can be safe from harm. I think that that should be the proper state of things in a healthy society. But I thought the question you were asking was whether it could ever be right to stop individual expression of opinion. Certainly it is commonly accepted that this is sometimes right. In wartime, for example, propaganda against the state is stopped, and in peace time propaganda liable to undermine morality. A man who incited others to commit murder would be arrested. Surely circumstances may arise when the situation is dangerous, and action has to be taken.

*Q*. No doubt such situations may arise, but again I don't

think you are quite meeting my point. Nearly everyone will agree that at certain times and in certain matters dangerous views may have to be suppressed, but the practical question is: Should not freedom be allowed, short of these extreme cases? In practice don't you think that tendencies may easily be branded as anti-social, when in fact they only threaten a particular kind of social order, which it would be better to get rid of?

*A.* Of course that may happen. I agree that in practice it is necessary to be quite sure that a tendency is gravely anti-social and really dangerous before suppression can be justified, and that what is threatened is a social system which is good. But all this seems rather wandering from the original question. We have come to agree that expression of individual opinion may sometimes be rightly suppressed, though normally it is better to allow as much freedom as possible—also that frequently opinion is suppressed wrongly or at least unnecessarily. However, all this seems rather obvious.

*Q.* The question this leads to and which many people would not think obvious, is that of religious tolerance and intolerance. I should like to hear your view on this. Do you think there is a right to freedom of religion?

*A.* I cannot answer yes or no, but again must make a great many distinctions. There are very many different circumstances which may affect the answer, and it depends on what kind of freedom is referred to.

*Q.* Well, should a man ever be forced to become a Catholic?

*A.* Certainly not. The Church teaches that very clearly indeed. A man can only be received into the Church if he desires this of his own free will and for the right reasons.

*Q.* Has not the Church approved of men being penalized for not being Catholics? Can this be right?

*A.* We must distinguish between the private beliefs a man holds and attempts he makes to spread these views. We must also distinguish between the Church itself and a Catholic state. A Catholic state might hold that it was its duty to protect its social system, based on Catholicism, which it believed to be a good social system, from dangerous propaganda liable to disrupt it.

*Q*. That seems reasonable as a quite general principle. But is there any country at the present day where these conditions exist?

*A*. There are a few countries which have a very large majority of Catholics. In special circumstances they might claim it was necessary to take measures to prevent a small minority endangering their system.

*Q*. What measures do you think they might take to do this?

*A*. If on the whole they were justified in taking measures of this kind, the general principle would apply that the measures should not be stricter than was necessary to make them effective. This question of tolerance has often been confused because people have not distinguished between the question whether suppression was justified, and the question whether particular means were justified. Barbarous methods were thought necessary to secure public order in the past, but there can be no doubt, whether it was right or wrong in the past, to employ them now would be very wrong indeed.

*Q*. Then are you saying that any country at the present day would be right in suppressing anti-Catholic propaganda?

*A*. All I have said is that under certain circumstances, which might exist at any time, it would be right. These circumstances have probably existed in the past, though that does not at all mean that the methods used were right. At the present day the situation is quite different. Of course if a group threatens to use violence and, if it gets into power, to suppress the Church, a Catholic state would have a right and duty to suppress it—if this was the best method of dealing with it. But I suppose you are referring to expression of opinion which is honest and only uses reasoning and persuasion, and itself advocates toleration? I should say that at the present time it would be wrong to suppress this.

*Q*. Why do you think there is such a difference between the present time and former times?

*A.* For one thing because in former times there were countries in which nearly all were Catholics, and this is hardly so today. But there is another reason. At the present day communication between one country and another is infinitely easier, and there are so many ways of distributing information that it is practically impossible to stop the expression of views —certainly not without a degree of police control which it would be impossible to justify. Measures of this kind could not be right, unless they could be really effective, and this seems impossible without causing more harm in other directions. Moreover at the present day news goes round the world at once, and suppression of anti-Catholic propaganda in a Catholic country would increase the suppression of Catholic propaganda elsewhere. It would mean that countries where Catholics were few would forbid the entrance of missionaries. I should say, then, that such action in a Catholic country would do far more harm than good to the Church as a whole at the present day, and for this reason alone would be wrong. Also history seems to show that a certain amount of opposition may have the excellent effect of keeping Catholics awake and vigorous, whereas, if they are protected from all opposition, they are apt to become slack. I repeat that, of course, if a party is trying to gain power which would forcibly suppress the Church and all it stands for, this is an entirely different situation. What I am saying is simply that to stop the expression of views opposed to the Church, if violence is not threatened, is likely to do the Church far more harm than good, and is therefore wrong. It is far more likely to help the Church if methods of persuasion are used, and any abuses which may be attacked are corrected.

*Q.* So you think there is no principle which forbids intolerance, but only expediency?

*A.* I don't think there is any principle which forbids a society to protect itself against propaganda which threatens its existence, provided it is a good society. If a nation is Catholic it has the right to suppress propaganda against the Church, if the danger is serious enough, and if it is not wiser—as would often be the case—to counter it by other methods. I think this is really an academic question, because such action would do more harm than good at the present day. It would be bound to cause the strongest prejudice against the Church among non-Catholics, and make it far harder for Catholics to get a hearing.

*Q.* Would not some of these arguments apply to intolerance in the past also?

*A.* Undoubtedly the rulers of the Church have not always acted wisely in their own interests. Indeed they have sometimes been their own worst enemies, forgetting that the good they were likely to do by a particular course of action was infinitely less than the harm they would certainly do.

*Q.* Is not the real argument against intolerance in religion that religion is not comparable to purely social movements? I mean this. It is justifiable for the state to take action against subversive tendencies, but can religious belief ever be subversive in the same way? Is it not always possible for a state to tolerate different religious beliefs without any real danger to itself?

*A.* This is no doubt true in the kind of conditions we are accustomed to in, say, England or the United States, and with the kind of religious controversies with which we are familiar. But the situation may be quite different, and far more violent passions may be aroused.

*Q.* But what right has one man to set himself up as the standard of what ought to be believed, if others honestly disagree?

*A.* Everyone must act on his own conviction of what is right. The fact that others disagree doesn't prove that a belief is wrong. Indeed any attitude a man takes up, even if he says the evidence on a given subject is inconclusive, is a positive attitude, and contradicts those who disagree. This need not lead to intolerance. Charity requires that everyone should be as tolerant as possible of others, because charity requires us to foster goodwill among mankind. Of course Catholics, believing their religion to be true, practise charity by trying to influence others towards belief, but it is through sympathy and understanding that this is likely to be done. On the other hand charity may sometimes require that force shall be met by force.

*Q.* I think the real question comes to this: Has a man a right to express his honest opinion and try to influence others, provided he is not going to be intolerant, if he gets the chance, towards those who differ from him?

*A.* He certainly has a right to hold any views he conscientiously holds—or, rather, no one has a right to interfere with his private views. If we believe his views are false we can hardly say, strictly speaking, that he has a right to hold them, as I have already argued, because we believe they are false. But a society which regards a man's views as harmful and dangerous may have a right to prevent expression of these views—or, rather, to be more accurate, it may have this right if we believe that the convictions held by the society in question are right and good.

*Q.* Why must we believe that our own views are true and all others false? Can't we hold that all such views are more or less provisional?

*A.* I should doubt whether many people would be willing to accept that. I should have thought that the highest type of character was based on convictions firmly held. Few people would think it right to hold as merely provisional such a principle as that we ought to help others and not lead a purely selfish life. I think the real dispute would be how far these convictions ought to go.

*Q.* Then does not this lead to a kind of law of the jungle, in which everyone must fight on behalf of his convictions? Isn't this a desperate conclusion?

*A.* We must reconcile ourselves, it seems to me, to the fact that different convictions are held about what is good for men. Mankind is composed of individuals, and the individual cannot get outside himself. He can try to understand why other people hold the views they do, but if, in the end, he finds his beliefs differ from theirs, he can only accept this as a regrettable fact. He cannot help regarding his own convictions as true and those which are in contradiction as false. He cannot regard it as right, taken as a principle, that men should be as free to spread false views as true ones.

*Q.* Is not this going to mean that society is bound to disintegrate through the struggle between opposing convictions?

*A.* Not necessarily, by any means. I have already argued that, even in a Catholic state and from the Catholic point of view, suppression of opposing views would not be justified, because it would not on the whole do good; it would not achieve its end. This, I think, is the situation in the modern world, and there seems no likelihood of the situation changing. If everyone would take this view, and no one threaten to use force against opponents, the practical result would be toleration.

*Q.* My difficulty is that you admit no principle of toleration.

*A.* I don't see how in the nature of the case there can be a principle of toleration in the sense you mean. It is simply a basic fact that men's beliefs differ, but you cannot think it right that a man should teach what you think wrong. We can agree to the general principle that a man should eat, but it is not right for him to eat food which is poisonous. When it is a question of teaching, the teaching may be true or false, good or bad.

*Q.* I don't think we shall get any further with this, but it leads to another question I should like to ask you. It is often said that thought should be free: do you think there is any important sense in which that is true?

*A.* Thought should certainly be free in the sense that all prejudice and influence which would be apt to keep us from the truth should be disregarded. The question is whether a particular influence or authority is good or bad, relevant or irrelevant.

*Q.* Doesn't it mean that we should not take for granted any influence or authority, but should examine its credentials with the greatest care?

*A.* Of course that is true. The question, as I said, is whether a particular influence or authority is reliable or not, whether it is part of the evidence for settling a given question, and we have to decide this ultimately by our own judgement. When opinions differ we have to decide for ourselves which we shall follow. All that can be said is that we ought to be intellectually honest.

*Q.* What do you mean by intellectual honesty?

*A.* I mean not deceiving ourselves, not persuading ourselves that we find an argument convincing when we do not find it convincing, but for some reason should like to do so, not letting emotion affect our judgement when it is irrelevant, and so on. Intellectual honesty means really trying to make truth our aim, and not allowing ourselves to shut our eyes to the evidence as it appears to us.

*Q.* Everybody would agree to that. But I suppose that the idea which supporters of "free thought" have at the back of their minds is that thought should be free from control by the Church, that in fact the Church has prevented the progress of knowledge.

*A.* To discuss this fully would involve an immense historical inquiry for which we have no time here. But I would point out that a believer regards religious truth as the supremely important kind of truth, and thinks that the Church has always proved a true guide here. Moreover we should have to weigh all that the Church has done for natural knowledge against what it has done to retard such knowledge. Once again we come back to the fact that men differ as to where truth lies. If we believe the Church we accept its teaching as a true guide.

*Q.* Yes, but is not this contradicted by the facts? Have not scholars and scientists proved right in a good many points in which at first they were strongly opposed by the Church? Was not evolution, for example, at first frowned on, though it is now accepted by the Church as quite compatible with her beliefs? Has not much progress been made in historical and scriptural questions, which was at first discouraged by the Church?

*A.* Everyone knows we must distinguish between the infallible teaching of the Church and the fallible teaching of the rulers of the Church. Undoubtedly the rulers of the Church have sometimes been unwise and misleading in their attitude to questions of science and scholarship.

*Q.* Doesn't it look, then, as though the supporters of free thought were not far wrong? They say that, if progress is to be made in science and scholarship, attention must not be paid to the Church's teaching. Does not this to a considerable extent turn out to be true?

*A.* We must get this matter clear, or else false conclusions will be drawn. In principle the only sense in which thought should be free is that it should not be prevented from reaching the truth. As to the various authorities it should, or should not, listen to, that depends on whether they are true guides or not. Catholics believe that the Church, when teaching officially, is a true guide on faith and morals. Even when the rulers of the Church do not speak infallibly, Catholics remember that in practice they may be prudent in hesitating to accept new theories until they are fully proved. Yet undoubtedly mistakes have sometimes been made with the result that progress in knowledge has been unnecessarily held back, and it is only honest to admit this. All we can say is that we believe that on the whole immensely more good than harm is done through the Church's guidance.

*Q.* This leads to a slightly different subject I should like to discuss. How does your theory apply to education? A child cannot decide what authority to accept. If a child is brought up as a Catholic, isn't this depriving him of his freedom to decide for himself? Didn't you say that, to realize his full personality, a man should make his own decision?

*A.* I said that a human person should be the true agent of his acts and not the mere instrument of others, for then his act is not really his own. It should be the outcome of his own reflection. It is only when a man is acting consciously and deliberately that he can be fully practising the Christian virtues.

A man could not be brainwashed into making a true act of the love of God. This, however, does not mean that good influence is not of the greatest value. I have explained my view about this—that it is not choice which matters, but that the important thing is that a man should possess the virtues, whether this is due to the influence of others or not.

*Q.* But I don't see how you can defend bringing up a child in the Catholic faith, when it cannot judge for itself, and when it is little more than an instrument in your hands.

*A.* If a child is to be instructed in any subject, it has first simply to accept what it is taught. It cannot judge for itself when it is a child. Instruction in religious knowledge only follows this general rule. If the parents are Catholics they naturally and rightly train their child in the Catholic faith, because they believe it to be true, and because they wish their child to receive the graces which the sacraments confer.

*Q.* Yes, but I still don't understand how the child is acting fully as a human person under such circumstances.

*A.* When a child is still young plainly it cannot act fully as a human person, whatever kind of knowledge we are talking about, whether science or history or any other subject. Religion is no exception. It is natural and inevitable that a child should accept what it is told. A child is on the way to becoming a fully mature person, but has not yet reached this state. It is not yet wholly separate from its parents, and the parents are right in teaching it what they believe to be true.

*Q.* Well, is not that equivalent to saying that it is inevitable and right that, to an important extent, human beings should be brainwashed?

*A.* No, surely not. When a man is brainwashed he is presumably like someone who is dreaming. A man, when he is awake, is himself the agent of his acts in a different way from a man who is dreaming. A child is the agent of its own acts in so far as it is awake, but it can be influenced from outside far more easily than a mature person. It comes to this. When a child accepts what it is taught, this is its own conscious act except in so far as the act is brought about by the influence of others rather than by its own reflection. The child really does accept what is taught it, whereas the brainwashed person only sees the teaching like a man in a dream.

*Q.* I still don't see why a child should not be left uncommitted in matters of religion till it grows up.

*A.* A child cannot be brought up in a quite neutral way with regard to religion, any more than it can with regard to science or history. After a certain time without training it becomes harder and harder to adapt itself and accept new ideas. Training or lack of training cannot be neutral. If the child is not brought up as a Catholic, its conduct becomes adjusted to a positive line which is different from that of a Catholic. It acquires habits of mind and thought which are positively Catholic or positively non-Catholic. No one can ever judge a question in a vacuum of complete impartiality, in the sense of having no previous principles or convictions affecting his view. All he can do is to make sure, to the best of his ability, that his principles and convictions are right and true.

*Q.* When the child grows up would it not be better for him to suspend his beliefs as far as possible, and do his best to look at the whole question impartially, however difficult this may be?

*A.* A person cannot give up his convictions at will and reconsider them from outside. If he is convinced he is convinced whether he likes it or not. It would be wrong to try and disbelieve what you believe to be true. A man can of course examine the evidence for his beliefs in an impartial spirit without giving up the beliefs.

*Q.* Surely it would be better, as far as possible, for a man to suspend his belief?

*A.* The person who has to answer this question is himself either a believer or a non-believer, and his belief or non-belief is bound to affect his answer, indeed to decide it. Plainly, a Catholic could not think it better to suspend belief, because he accepts the Church as true, and believes faith is a gift of

God, and that providence is directing the course of events, if no sin is committed.

*Q*. But what becomes of all you have said about the value of a fully human act?

*A*. The theory I have defended is that a fully human act need not be an act of choice. An act of belief in the Christian religion must certainly be an act made by the person himself, not merely through the influence of others, but accepted as his own with consciousness of its meaning and implications. But that is fully compatible with the act's being the outcome of God's grace. Choice may or may not enter in, and may enter in to a greater or a less extent, but choice, I have suggested, as such is only an unfortunate necessity. An act is not fully a human act because it is an act of choice.

*Q*. Why should not the scientific approach be the right one? There can't of course be experiments and tests in religious matters, but why should not the evidence be judged with the same absolute detachment and impartiality?

*A*. Everyone must agree that evidence should be looked at as it really presents itself, in the best way to appreciate its truth. But evidence is of very different kinds. The evidence for Christianity and the Catholic faith is, in part at least, very different from the kind of evidence that a scientist deals with. In so far as it is the same kind of evidence as a scientist deals with it should certainly be dealt with in the same way. So far, for example, as it consists in historical facts, they should be examined like other historical facts, and so too with archaeological and scientific facts. But that is only one side of the evidence. From one point of view the evidence consists in the appeal which the doctrines and practice of the Catholic religion make to a man's spiritual ideals and aspirations. He has to ask himself whether this way of life and thought satisfies him and rings true—whether it carries with it a sense of duty and obligation to him. It is considerations of this kind which can enable the merely objective evidence to bring final, personal, conviction.

*Q.* I think I understand what you mean.

*A.* I should like to make a final remark about tolerance and intolerance because it is easily misunderstood. In one sense tolerance is meaningless—in so far as it implies that you should not regard as right and true what in fact you do regard as right and true. But in the looser and more general sense in which the word is used toleration is a true ideal. All should try to understand the position of others and to see the good and truth which we can almost always accept as present in the beliefs of those with whom in certain respects we disagree. All should treat the honest convictions of others, even when they believe them to be false, with a proper deference. There is a Christian tolerance which is certainly a virtue.

# SELECT BIBLIOGRAPHY

AQUINAS, St Thomas: *Summa Theologica*, 3 vols, translated by Fathers of the English Dominican Province, London, Burns Oates, and New York, Benziger, 1948.

BIVORT DE LA SAUDÉE, Jacques de (Editor): *God, Man and the Universe*, "The Problem of Evil", by Yves M. J. Congar, London, Burns Oates, and New York, Kenedy, 1954.

CRONIN, C. J.: *The Science of Ethics*, Volume I, Dublin, Gill, 1909.

DANIÉLOU, J., S.J.: *The Lord of History*, translated by N. J. Abercrombie, London, Longmans, and Chicago, Regnery, 1958.

D'ARCY, M. C., S.J.: *The Sense of History, Secular and Sacred*, London, Faber, and New York, Harper, 1959; *The Pain of this World and the Providence of God*, London and New York, Longmans, 1953.

FARRELL, Walter, O.P.: *A Companion to the Summa*, Volume I, London and New York, Sheed and Ward, 1941.

GARRIGOU-LAGRANGE, R., O.P.: *Providence*, St Louis, Herder, 1937.

JOYCE, G. H., S.J.: *Principles of Natural Theology*, London and New York, Longmans, 1923.

MARITAIN, Jacques: *On the Philosophy of History*, London, Bles, 1959, and New York, Scribner, 1957.

PATTERSON, R. L.: *The Conception of God in the Philosophy of Aquinas*, London, Allen and Unwin, 1935.

PHILLIPS, R. P.: *Modern Thomistic Philosophy*, Volume II, London, Burns Oates, 1934, and Westminster, Md, Newman Press, 1945.

RASHDALL, Hastings: *The Theory of Good and Evil*, London and New York, Oxford Univ. Press, 1924.

SMITH, G. D. (Editor): *The Teaching of the Catholic Church*, London, Burns Oates, and New York, Macmillan, 1947.

# The Twentieth Century Encyclopedia of Catholicism

*The number of each volume indicates its place in the over-all series and not the order of publication.*

**PART ONE: KNOWLEDGE AND FAITH**

1. What Does Man Know?
2. Is Theology a Science?
3. The Meaning of Tradition
4. The Foundations of Faith
5. Does the Faith Change?
6. What is Faith?
7. God's Word to Man
8. Myth or Mystery?
9. What is a Miracle?
10. Is There a Christian Philosophy?
11. Early Christian Philosophy
12. Medieval Christian Philosophy
13. Modern Thought and Christian Philosophy
14. Does Christianity Oppose Science?
15. The God of Reason

**PART TWO: THE BASIC TRUTHS**

16. The Worship of God
17. What is the Trinity?
18. The Holy Spirit
19. In the Hands of the Creator
20. The Problem of Evil
21. Who is the Devil?
22. Freedom and Providence
23. The Theology of Grace
24. The Word Made Flesh
25. What is Redemption?
26. The Communion of Saints
27. The Basic Virtues
28. Life After Death

## PART THREE: THE NATURE OF MAN
29. The Origins of Man
30. Evolution
31. What is Man?
32. What is Life?
33. What is Psychology?
34. Man in His Environment
35. What is Metaphysics?
36. Psychical Phenomena

## PART FOUR: THE MEANS OF REDEMPTION
37. Prayer
38. The Nature of Mysticism
39. Spiritual Writers of the Early Church
40. Christian Spirituality of the Middle Ages
41. Post-Reformation Spirituality
42. Spirituality in Modern Times
43. What are Indulgences?
44. Mary The Mother of God
45. The Marian Cult
46. What is a Saint?
47. What is an Angel?

## PART FIVE: THE LIFE OF FAITH
48. What is the Church?
49. What is a Sacrament?
50. Christian Initiation
51. The Forgiveness of Sins
52. What is the Eucharist?
53. What is a Priest?
54. Christian Marriage
55. The Death of a Christian
56. Christian Morality
57. Christian Social Teaching
58. World Morality
59. Christianity and Money

## PART SIX: THE WORD OF GOD
60. What is the Bible?
61. The Promised Land
62. Biblical Archeology
63. Biblical Criticism
64. God's People in the Bible
65. The Religion of Israel
66. Messianic Prophecies
67. How Do We Know Jesus?
68. The Life of Our Lord
69. What is the Good News?
70. St. Paul and His Message

71. What the Old Testament Does Not Tell Us
72. What the Gospels Do Not Tell Us
73. The Jewish Faith

PART SEVEN: THE HISTORY OF THE CHURCH
74. The Revolution of the Cross
75. The Dawn of the Middle Ages
76. The Early Middle Ages
77. The Later Middle Ages
78. Reformation and Counter-Reformation
79. The Church in the Modern Age

PART EIGHT: THE ORGANIZATION OF THE CHURCH
80. What is Canon Law?
81. The Papacy
82. The Government of the Church
83. Successors of the Apostles
84. The Christian Priesthood
85. Religious Orders of Men
86. Religious Orders of Women
87. The Laity's Place in the Church
88. The Catholic Spirit

PART NINE: THE CHURCH AND THE MODERN WORLD
89. Church and State
90. The Church in World Economy
91. Contemporary Atheism
92. Science and Religion
93. Christianity and Psychiatry
94. Christianity and the Machine Age
95. Christianity and the Space Age
96. Christianity and Communism
97. Christianity and Colonialism
98. The Church Works through Her Saints
99. History of the Missions
100. Missions in Modern Times
101. Religious Sociology
102. The Mission of the Church in the World
103. The Church and Sex
104. The Workers of the Church
105. Charity in Action
106. Christianity and Education
107. Why We Believe

PART TEN: THE WORSHIP OF THE CHURCH
108. The Spirit of Worship
109. The Books of Worship
110. History of the Mass
111. The Mass in the West
112. Eastern Liturgies

113. The Church's Calendar
114. Vestments and Church Furniture

**PART ELEVEN: CATHOLICISM AND LITERATURE**
115. What is a Christian Writer?
116. Sacred Languages
117. Christian Humanism
118. Christianity and Modern Thought
119. Modern Christian Literature

**PART TWELVE: CATHOLICISM AND THE ARTS**
120. The Christian Meaning of Art
121. The Origins of Christian Art
122. Church Building
123. Christian Painting and Sculpture
124. Christian Theatre
125. Christian Music
126. Motion Pictures, Radio and Television

**PART THIRTEEN: CATHOLICISM AND SCIENCE**
127. Embryo and Anima
128. Nuclear Physics in Peace and War
129. Medicine and Morals
130. To be assigned
131. To be assigned
132. To be assigned
133. To be assigned

**PART FOURTEEN: OUTSIDE THE CHURCH**
134. Judaism and the Law
135. Greek and Russian Orthodoxy
136. Heresies and Heretics
137. Protestantism
138. The Ecumenical Movement
139. Modern Sects

**PART FIFTEEN: NON-CHRISTIAN BELIEFS**
140. Primitive Religions
141. Religions of the Ancient East
142. Greco-Roman Religion
143. The Religion of Mohammed
144. Hinduism
145. Buddhism
146. Mystery Cults
147. Superstition
148. The Rationalists

**PART SIXTEEN: GENERAL AND SUPPLEMENTARY VOLUMES**
149. Why I am a Christian
150. Index

*All titles are subject to change.*